SCOTTISH CUSTOMS

Sheila Livingstone

Birlinn

First published in Great Britain, 1996, by
Birlinn Limited
14 High Street
Edinburgh EH1 1TE

British Library Cataloguing-in-Publication Data
A Catalogue record of this book is available
from the British Library.

ISBN 1 874744 41 6

Designed and typeset in 10/12pt Horley Old Style
by Janet Watson

Made and printed in Finland by
Werner Söderström OY

CONTENTS

INTRODUCTION

*A*n act becomes a custom when it is carried out regularly on the appropriate occasion until by force of habit people adopt it. The original meaning or reason for the act may have become obscured yet the act itself is perpetuated and it is considered bad manners for people not to behave in the expected way. Customs arise as a mark of respect, an aversion of ill-luck and as a bringer of good luck and success. Some may be exclusive to one area while others are found nationally and internationally in one form or another.

Many customs are used as part of ritual. Some form part of ceremonies considered rites of passage – birth, marriage, death while others are essential items in festivals often held annually, at specific times, as they have been for centuries. Customs can be old or fairly new. Their origin can be buried in tradition or can spring spontaneously from modern behaviour to take their place in common ritual. The Mexican Wave is now regularly seen at sporting events. It is a mystery who starts this movement and how everyone else responds. In the same way the laying of flowers at the spot where an accident or death had occurred is becoming common. This custom is taken further in Europe where roadside shrines are built in memoriam with flowers constantly replaced.

Many customs can be traced back to the Druids. The natural world teemed with life: animals, stones, plants, rivers and wells were endowed with feelings which mankind had to respect and come to terms with. In Scotland, especially in the Highlands and Islands, these customs were so firmly held in the hearts and minds of the people that when Christianity was established the Church of Rome integrated and sanctified them. It slowly drew them in by renaming the places of devotion after saints and allowing old festivals to continue with a veneer of Christianity overlaid on them. The magical powers believed to be associated with specific places were transferred, their powers now attributed to God. The old runes used in charms were altered to become blessings in the name of the Virgin Mary or the Trinity of Father, Son and Holy Ghost.

It is interesting to note that after the Reformation when folk of Lowland Scotland mainly became Presbyterians they managed to despise things Roman which they called popish, but could happily reconcile the duality of retaining pagan customs in tandem with their new faith. The Church of Scotland and the Episcopalian Church often tried to ban these customs as heathenish but people persisted in their habits, maintaining a sort of dual insurance just in case they might give offence to the old gods and suffer as a result.

Many Scots lived in a state of continual fear, preached at every Sunday about hell and damnation:

> *The doctrine taught concerning Satan, his motives and influence in the beginning of this century supplied the popular mind with reasons to account for almost all the evils, public and private, which befell society; and as the observed ills of life, real or imaginary, greatly outnumbered the observed good occurrences, the thought of Satan was more constantly before the people's minds than was the thought of God.*
>
> Folklore or Superstitious Beliefs in the West of Scotland
> within this Century, James Napier, 1879

The Church frowned upon dancing and frivolity, religion being pessimistic and severe. Any misdemeanour would result in Godly retribution and punishment by the elders in front of the congregation. Unsurprisingly, then, people joined in celebrations where they could drink and let their hair down without the heavy hand of authority descending upon them.

Customs can become an obsession, props to take the blame for all ills. In ritual there is security. One of the severest punishments for disobedience in pagan Celtic times was to be banned from taking part in ritual. In those far-off days the people were controlled by those who were privy to the magic incantations and passed on their knowledge only to a chosen few just before their death. Today the world seems smaller, communication easier and religion no longer the mainstay of society in Scotland that it once was, even if that was through fear, and yet many people still cling to the remnants of the old Scottish customs as to a favourite toy or shawl.

Sheila Livingstone, 1995

BIRTH

*A*lthough families tended to be large up until the twentieth century, few survived intact. Many children died, at birth, in infancy and childhood from infectious diseases, and during the teenage years from illnesses such as tuberculosis. Those who leapt those hurdles, especially boys, might be killed in the army, down the pit or at sea, while daughters were often lost giving birth. Big families compensated for this loss and some adults did live into their eighties and nineties.

The announcement of a happy event was greeted with delight by the women of the community. No matter whether it be the first or the eighth, a new baby was a welcome diversion. Until the 1970s few men ever attended the birth of their offspring voluntarily; it was women's business and they ensured that all the correct customs were carried out, not only to protect the child from evil influence, but also to protect the community.

Childbirth was a rite of passage which troubled people who considered it a crack in time which left the moment open to evil influences. Objects which might absorb evil were put out of the house and animals were also evicted. Bottles were uncorked and mirrors covered in case the baby's image might be taken by the fairies. It was also believed that the baby seeing itself in a mirror or picture frame glass could cause rickets. This idea perhaps stems from the distorted image made by some mirrors.

Fertility

From the moment that a bride was married, custom decreed that everything should be done to encourage fertility. A willow branch was placed beneath the bridal bed, rice was thrown and all knots untied so that there would be no restrictions to prevent pregnancy. She was given a chamber pot filled with salt with a doll in it to represent a baby.

From the time of her marriage the new wife was watched for signs that she might be pregnant and if this did not occur within the first few months, she became the subject of relentless gossip. It was usually assumed to be the woman's fault unless someone had tied a knot in her husband's handkerchief, unknown to him, at the time of the wedding. Sometimes the fairies were blamed for having placed a curse on the woman, perhaps because the couple's house was built over fairy territory. However it was the wife who took steps to right the matter.

Aids to conception

In some areas there were stones or rocks which had natural holes through them usually made by the weather. The wife had to crawl through this chanting a blessing to Bride, the goddess or saint of childbirth. At Glenavon, near Braemar, women embraced a certain stone for the same purpose and in other areas they put their arms around an oak tree. Some believed that smelling flowers and eating the fruit from trees could encourage pregnancy. The importance of trees stems from the Druids who worshipped them because they believed that the spirits of the dead returned to live in trees.

In the eighteenth century, at Fochabers, Moray, on St Mary's Day in August an auld wife, a cailleach, knelt on a particular flat stone. The women who wanted to have babies, but were having problems conceiving, gathered there and took off their shoes and stockings, rolled up their skirts and petticoats to expose their wombs and went sunwise round the auld wife, who threw cold spring water at them. Next they exposed their breasts and repeated the process.

On the same day in Mull barren women walked around a well three times sunwise then drank the water.

Once pregnant it was supposed to be possible to determine the sex of the baby by holding a needle on a thread over the mother's womb. If it swung round in a circle it indicated that the baby would be a girl and if it swung backwards and forwards it would be a boy.

St Bride

Rocking an empty cradle or placing a doll into one might help fertility. The women sat knitting while singing lullabies and rocking the cradle, beseeching Bride to bring springtime.

> O Bride, Brideag, come with the wand
> To this wintry land;
> And breathe with the breath of Spring so bland,
> Bride, Bride, Little Bride;

Traditional

This reflects the custom long carried out on St Bride's Day, February the first or thirteenth depending which calendar was in use, of bedding a straw figure bedecked with flowers and shells, sometimes made from the last sheaf cut at the previous harvest, dedicated to Bride and known as the Brideag. After twelve maidens in white had taken her round the township the Brideag was bedded, with all the luck that she is supposed to bring.

Easing the pain

There were many customs and beliefs about ways of easing the mother's pain at childbirth. Her husband could walk seven times around the house sunwise or deaseil (the numbers three, seven and nine have always been considered lucky). This occurs in many customs and is supposed to ward off evil influences.

Another prized charm was a seed which was carried across the Atlantic by the Gulf Stream and could be picked up on the shores of the west coast. It was called the Virgin's Nut because it has a faint mark of a cross on its kidney shape. This nut was often blessed by the Catholic priests on the Western Isles and given to women in labour to hold in their hand to ease pain and ensure safe delivery.

Clutching a piece of coral or some red rowan berries was also believed to relieve her pain as coral was regarded by the Romans as a guard against evil and rowans were considered both magical and sacred in Scotland. Midwives used to sprinkle urine over the mother-to-be with the same intent and, similarly, amber beads threaded on red silk were favoured by the rich as a charm.

> He's pu'ed her a bunch of yon red roddins
> That grew beside yon thorn,
> But an a drink o' water clear,
> Intill his drinking horn.
>> Willie o' Douglas Dale, *traditional ballad*

A pair of the father's trousers or a Bible was placed beneath the pillow of the delivery bed to relieve the pain.

Shooting

In the days of bows and arrows it was customary that an arrow was fired from east to west, thus carrying the pain away and then the quiver would be left empty; in later centuries a gun was fired and all guns in the house would have their cartridges removed.

> When ye hear me give a cry,
> Ye'll shoot your bow and let me lie.
>> *Leesome Brand*, traditional ballad

St Bride aids childbirth

Bride or St Bride was also associated with easing childbirth, since she was believed to be the handmaiden who assisted the Virgin Mary in the stable at Bethlehem as Jesus was born. To solicit her aid the midwife went to the door of the house, stood on the step with her hands against the jambs and called out softly:

> *Bride! Bride! come in,*
> *Thy welcome is truly made,*
> *Give thou relief to the woman,*
> *And give the conception to the Trinity*
>
> Traditional

If Bride hears the plea she will help the woman in labour deliver a fine, healthy child.

Charms against prolonging the birth

The fairies, it was believed by all classes, were ever watchful for the opportunity to seize the baby and substitute it with a changeling. Several customs kept the fairies away, at the moment of birth. The petals or leaves of the pearlwort or mothan (as it was also called) were placed behind the mother's right knee which kept fairies from entering and interfering with the birth. The bonnet of the father was placed on the bed and a cross of rowan beside the Bible over the bed. If the bedstead was not made of iron, which was revered for its magical properties, then a nail or an iron object such as a smoothing iron was placed under the bed.

If labour was prolonged, as was often the case, all the women present would circle the bed waving the Bible in the air, bidding all enemies to go to the Red Sea. The reason for this was that fairies or witches were suspected of having managed to gain a lock of hair from the mother or a paring of her nail or her left shoe, and had thereby put an enchantment upon her.

> *Trefoil, vervain, St John's-wort, dill,*
> *Hinders witches of their will;*
> *Weel is them, that weel may*
> *Fast upon St Andrew's Day.*
>
> *Saint Bride and her brat,*
> *Saint Colme and his cat,*

Saint Michael and his spear,
Keep the house frae reif and wear.
        Guy Mannering, Sir Walter Scott, 1829

Another interpretation was that those who had committed infidelity always had a hard labour and there would be gossip and suspicion if it were not the first baby.

It was believed that a witch could arrest childbirth by having a ball of black thread in a black bag as she placed a curse on the mother-to-be. Wonderful tales were told of prolonged deliveries with babies arriving complete with beard.

To release the mother from the enchantment the bed was moved over the spot where a chest or any other piece of furniture made of red rowan had stood. Or counter-charms would release them and bring about a safe delivery.

O wha has loosed the nine witch-knots,
That were amang that ladye's locks?
And wha's ta'en out the kames o' care,
That were amang the ladye's hair:
And wha's ta'en down that bush o' woodbine,
That hung between her bower and mine?
And wha has killed the master-kid
That ran beneath that ladye's bed?
And wha has loosed her left foot shoe,
And let that ladye lighter be?
        Willie's Ladye, traditional ballad

On the Isle of Arran when it was suspected that an enchantment had been placed on the mother-to-be, gold rings or pieces of silver and gold were put into a basin of water fresh from the well. She was given three mouthfuls of this to drink in the name of the Father, Son and Holy Ghost and delivery was almost immediate.

The moment of birth

The birthing was called the 'cryin' and was the signal for more activity. Immediately the baby was born the howdie or midwife put a teaspoonful of salt in its mouth. In some parts of the Highlands a ball of butter was used instead and elsewhere it was a teaspoonful of earth laced with whisky or gin but they all served the same purpose, to safeguard the baby from the fairies.

At one time the baby was taken immediately to a running stream or a pool and dipped into the water. This was supposed to make the child strong and healthy. Latterly the baby's first bath was in front of a fire, preferably of rowan twigs, and in water in which a silver coin or a gold ring had been placed to ensure wealth. Sometimes salt was added to the water and the baby made to taste it three times before the mother's breasts were also washed with the salty brine. Milk is also recorded as being used to purify the baby against evil spirits, following the belief that Mary was supposed to have bathed the baby Jesus in milk. Babies born in autumn were often given honey and the milk of the hazelnut as their first food.

A dish containing oatmeal and water was offered to each woman present at the birth and she had to sup three spoonfuls to bring protection to the house and its occupants.

Birthmarks

Birthmarks were attributed to the behaviour of the mother during pregnancy. She must never step over a grave or be frightened by a hare or other creature or the mark would take the shape of whatever had influenced the mother in an evil way.

Time

The time of birth was also of great interest, certain days being more favourable than others, those born on different days of the week supposedly exhibiting different characteristics.

Monday's child is fair of face,
Tuesday's child is full of grace,
Wednesday's child is full of woe,
Thursday's child has far to go.
Friday's child is loving and giving,

Saturday's child works hard for a living,
But the child that is born on the Sabbath day,
Is blithe and bonny and good and gay.

Traditional

Astrologers noted exact details of the positions of the stars at the moment of birth to predict the baby's future. Babies born at the time of an incoming tide were supposed to have an easier life than those born at an ebb tide, while those babies born under a waxing moon would have more prosperity than those under a waning one.

The gypsies had other means of divining the future of a baby. Wool spun from three different colours, white, grey and black was entwined by use of the distaff and spindle while reciting a charm.

Twist ye, twine ye! even so,
Mingle shades of joy and woe,
Hope and fear, and peace and strife,
In the thread of human life.

While the mystic twist is spinning,
And the infant's life beginning,
Dimly seen through twilight bending,
Lo, what varied shapes attending.

Passions wild, and follies vain,
Pleasures soon exchanged for pain,
Doubt and jealousy, and fear,
In the magic dance appear.

Now they wax, and now they dwindle,
Whirling with the whirling spindle,
Twist ye, twine ye! even so,
Mingle human bliss and woe.

Guy Mannering, Sir Walter Scott, 1829

Born lucky

A sign of certain luck was for a baby to be born with a caul or membrane covering its face. This or being born the seventh child of a seventh child often indicated that the infant would grow up to have the second sight. Those born between midnight and one o'clock in the morning were supposed to be able to see ghosts while those born on Christmas Day would never see one.

The protective use of fire

The domestic fire was originally found in the centre of the room immediately below the opening which acted as a chimney. Fire gave heat and also light. Stemming from the Druidical tradition that fire was a power against evil and cleansed everything which came in contact with it the baby was often handed backwards and forwards three times across the flames. Or the new baby was placed in a basket on top of cheese and bread wrapped in a linen cloth which the oldest person present then had to carry three times around the fire and suspend for a few seconds on the swee above the flames. Bread, because of its sacramental use, was considered as a protection against evil. The food was then divided amongst the company to ensure good health in the coming year.

If no fire was available the midwife would wrap a straw rope over an iron hoop, such as those which are used to bind a barrel. The straw was set on fire with paraffin and two women held it vertically while the baby was passed through the hoop three times. The midwife might also carry a lit peat on a shovel three times around the mother.

Afterbirth

The Celts believed that the afterbirth contained the soul and must be treated with respect. The midwife took the afterbirth and buried it. If a tree planted at the spot grew straight and had lots of foliage it meant that the child would be healthy and prosperous. The cord was also treated as an omen. If, put away in a drawer, it remained moist this was a good sign but if it shrivelled up it signified ill-health and even an early death.

Cryin cheese and groaning malt

When a safe delivery was accomplished there was rejoicing but only the womenfolk were allowed to attend the first celebration. This kenno, or ancient custom, was supposed to be carried out in secret by the women of the family without the knowledge of the men, especially of the father. He, on reaching the birth chamber, had to offer refreshments to the gossips who attended the birth. They in turn had to refuse. Then, when he had gone the cryin cheese and the groaning malt (cheese and ale made specially to be taken to wish health to the new baby) were produced by the women of the family and everyone ate and drank their fill. The remainder was divided amongst them and, still observing secrecy, they took their portion home. Kimmerins, in Galloway and cummerfalls in the east were other names for this celebration. At this feast the cryin bannock made of oatmeal, milk and sugar and baked in a frying pan was also eaten.

Wetting the baby's head

Not to be outdone, the men had their own celebration which was usually referred to as wetting the baby's head. Many a child should be well blessed if the amount of liquor drunk bestowed luck. In fishing communities the father sent a bottle of whisky down to the boat to his fellow crewmen so that they might toast the baby's health.

Cummers feast

On the fourth week after the lady's delivery she is sett on her bed on a low footstool, the bed is covered with some neat pieces of white satin, with three pillows at her back covered with the same, she is in full dress with a lapped headdress and a fan in her hand. Having informed her aquaintance what day she is to see company, they all come and pay their respects to her standing or walking a little throw the room (for there were no chairs). They drink a glass of wine and eat a bit of cake and then give

place to others. Towards the end of the week all the
friends were asked to the Cummers feast. This was a
supper where every gentleman brought a pint of wine to
be drunk by him and his wife. The supper was a ham at
the head, and a pyrimid of fowl at the bottom. The dish
consisted of four or five ducks, hens in the middle and
partridge above. There was an eating posset in the
middle of the table, with dried fruits and sweetmeats at
the sides. When they had finished their supper, the meat
was removed and in a momemt everybody flew to the
sweatmeats to pocket them; upon which a scramble
insued, chairs overturned, and everything on the table,
warsalling and pulling at one another with the utmost
noise. When all was quiet they went to the stoups (for
there were no bottles), of which the women had a good
share. For though it was a disgrace to be seen drunk,
yet it was none to be a little intoxicate in good company.
A few days later this same company was invited to the
christening which was allwise in church, all in high dress,
a number of them young ladies who were called maiden
cummers. One of them presented the child to the father.
After the ceremony they dined and supped together and
the night often concluded with a ball.

Caldwell Papers, Elizabeth Mure, 1750

High born

Great celebrations took place on the birth of the son and heir
of a chieftain or on the occasion of a royal birth.

On the birth of the prince, afterwards Charles the Second,
which took place between eleven and twelve this forenoon,
the Lyon King at Arms was despatched by the King from
London, to carry the news to Scotland. The Lyon arrived
in Edinburgh on the third day therafter, June 1st, when
immediately cannon were shot, bells rung and a table
spread in the High Street, between the Cross and the
Tron, for two hundred persons, including the nobility,

Privy Council and judges, the company being waited on
by the heralds and trumpeters in their official dress.

> Domestic Annals of Scotland, Vol 2, From the Reformation
> to the Revolution, Robert Chambers, n.d.

Problems

However everything did not always work out well. Many mothers and babies died in childbirth,the mother often from puerpal or childbed fever. To prevent this the midwife wound a blue thread around the mother's finger, sometimes the same thread which had been used by her mother and grandmother.

If a baby died its clothes, toys and cradle were burned and not used for another child as the bad luck could be transferred. It is still common for people to place a deposit on a baby's pram and cot but not to collect it until after the baby's safe arrival.The idea of tempting fate is so strong that some people go further and will not decorate a room or have everything ready until all is well.

Baptism

Forms of baptism existed before Christianity. A person's name was equated with their soul by the Celts and a naming ceremony legitimised it and guaranteed their inheritance.

The custom became of utmost importance after Christianity was established in Scotland. Should a baby die unbaptised it was considered a heathen and could not be buried within the churchyard. In some areas it was believed that such babies became earthbound and appeared as ghosts. Stillbirths were also treated in this way. Although clerical baptism was recommended within eight days, in rural areas it could be some time before a priest or clergyman was in the district and kirk session minutes often record a considerable time between birth and baptism. Midwives therefore always tried to carry out a ceremony of baptism called lay or birth-baptism. Three drops of water in the name of the Father,

Son and Holy Ghost sprinkled on the baby's forehead would sanctify the baby and protect it from fairies and evil. Sometimes spittle was used as it has always been considered to have magical powers.

Once again most people did not see anything untoward about mixing religion and the supernatural. Fairies were accepted as fact by the Church and even Presbyterians believed in their existence just as they believed in witchcraft. There were many customs regarded as vital for the health and prosperity of the child. The godparent should be an unmarried girl, a cummer or kimmer who should carry the child to the church.

Setting out

This was often the baby and the mother's first outing. Before leaving the house the baby was carried up a few stairs so that it might prosper. If no stair was available a ladder or chair would do. The mother was a target for fairies who tried to lure mothers to fairyland to nurse fairy children and and she was at risk until she was kirked, as her first visit to the church after the birth was called. It was lucky to throw a hot peat or a live coal after her to ward off the fairies as she walked to the church. On arrival she walked three times sunwise around the church with the christening party.

Naming the child

No one called the child by its Christian name until its baptism. Sometimes the minister found the name written on a piece of paper pinned to the baby's shawl, or it was whispered to him at the last minute. It was generally the custom to call the first baby after its paternal grandparents, the next after the maternal and the rest using family names. One Scottish custom which seems to have died out is that of adding *ina* to the father's name to feminise it. There were many a Robina, Jamesina, Thomasina, Edwina, Georgina and Williamina in Scotland. They generally called themselves just Ina. Roberta or Bertha were also favoured.

The first person to meet the christening party had to be offered food. By rights to complete the custom the recipient should accept and say "God bless the bairn".

Christenings often took place at the manse or in the home of the child. In 1690 private baptisms were frowned upon by the re-established Presbyterian Church and the General Assembly insisted that all children must be baptised during public worship, as is usually the case in Presbyterian churches today.

Some clergy interpreted the law so closely that they stated that it were better a child should die unbaptised than the law be broken. Others were less dictatorial and announced from the pulpit that they would hold a public worship at a remote cottage or farmtown and there they carried out the baptism before a gathering of friends and family. Nevertheless kirk sessions began to charge fines which they put in the poorbox if the baptism was not performed within the church.

The Kirk Session ordained that whoever sends for the minister to marry or baptize out of the church shall pay for each marriage 20/- and for each baptism 10/- Scots.
Minutes of the Kirk Session of Drymen, 1696

Over the iron

Long after the Reformation the Presbyterian Church was angrily banning an age-old custom of taking the baby to the local blacksmith for an "owre iron" christening to guard against the fairies. In many old session registers admonishments are recorded of parents being fined for having contravened the teaching of the Kirk. These same parents usually brought the baby to the church to be baptised but also wanted the safety net of the traditional ceremony.

Fonts and christening gowns

Although plain stone fonts had been in use for centuries more ornate stone and marble fonts for baptising infants became a part of church decor especially during the competitive building period after the Disruption of 1843 and in the

Victorian era. It was in this era that christening gowns became elaborate and showy. These were often made of fine lawn with Ayrshire embroidery, which is delicate white threadwork. Many are still in existence and still used for baptism.

Baptismal water

If there were several babies being baptised, as was often the case in outlying areas, the water for baptism, if it were used for a male child, had to be changed for a female in case she might develop facial hair or masculine leanings while those baptised by the same water were said to become life-long friends. If a female baby cried it was considered that the couple's next baby would be a boy. In the Middle Ages the right hand of a male child was not baptised, as an unhallowed blow to the enemy was considered lethal.

If the baby's eyes were bathed with baptismal water it would never see a ghost. Many people kept the water in a bottle as they considered that it had magical properties. The night of the christening the baby remained unbathed so that it could sleep under the protection of the Holy water.

In the Church of Scotland the act of baptism incorporates acceptance of responsibility by the congregation for the child's Christian upbringing and its name is entered on the cradle roll of the church in which the sacrament takes place.

Celebrations

An Act of Parliament in 1617 legalised the selling into slavery of children of the poor. Under this Act a child was contracted out to a master to work for him until he was thirty years of age. The workers at the salt-pans of the collieries were coerced into binding over their babies at birth by the custom of giving arles.

There existed the strange practice of binding their infants over to their master at the time of baptism, in the presence of the minister and neighbours as witnesses; and when a thriftless collier was in sore need of money to defray

christening festivities, he often sold the freedom of his son
to the employer, who gave arles or earnest money to the
father promising to provide his baby serf with a garden and
house and protection in sickness and age. From that hour
the arled child was recognised as bound for life to the pit.

The Social Life of Scotland in the 18th Century, H.G. Graham, 1899

As with funeral rites baptismal celebration could get out of hand.
The Church once again tried to discourage such behaviour.

The too great gatherings at some baptisms, too great
preparations made for them, and too much drunk at them,
and in some places there is a scandalous way at drinking
in coming with the child to and from the place of
administration, whereas at such time, not only parents
should endeavour a religious frame of soul, but also any
friends and neighbours that are invited upon such an
occasion to be witnesses to the dedication should be devout.

Records of the Presbytery of Penpont, 1736.

Cradles and charms

The wood which was used to make a baby's cradle was one of
the sacred ones. Elder was popular, as were rowan and oak.
Iron nails were used and it was luckier to borrow a cradle than
use a new one. A sprig of mistletoe, preferably gathered on the
sixth day of the new moon, was often placed in a cradle or
strands of convolvulus burned at both ends were hung over it
to ward off the fairies. The father's dirk was laid in the cradle
and became a protective symbol because of the cross made by
the junction of the handle and the blade. The baby was
sometimes given a bracelet of coral or a simple daisychain to
wear in order to give an added protection.

The bairnie she stryled in linen so fine,
In a gilded cradle she laid it syne,
Mickle saut and light she laid therin,
Cause yet in God's House it had'na been.

The King's Daughter, traditional ballad

When a cradle needs to be moved during a flitting a pillow was placed in it to keep the mother safe from harm.

The custom of hanging moving objects, which often rattle, across a cradle, cot or pram to amuse the baby originates from the idea that noise frightens away evil spirits.

Changelings

For centuries the fear of a healthy baby being spirited away was very real to the country folk. . . If a child was born retarded or physically deformed in any way the immediate reaction was to declare that it had been taken and replaced by a changeling. If it cried all the time and refused to suck this was a sign that somehow not enough precautions had been taken and the fairies had entered the house and spirited the baby away.

The fairies took human babies because they had to sacrifice a child to the devil every seven years and rather than lose their own children they stole human ones. It was also believed that older children were still vulnerable and if they showed signs of wasting away or of diseases such as infantile paralysis, deformed bones or mental illness that was proof that a substitution had been made.

Keeping an open Bible near the baby when it was left alone or placing a knitting needle or a large iron pin in the cradle or burning leather on the fire should keep the fairies at bay. Hanging a pair of the father's trousers over the baby's cradle at night or a pair of scissors opened so that they formed a cross were other ploys. The child's nails or hair were never cut before it was a year old and if this did happen then great care had to be taken to burn the clippings so that no fairy could steal them and exert an evil influence over the child. The first cutting after one year should be made over an open Bible.

It was considered wise to watch the baby night and day, in the same way as they watched the corpse at a wake. The bed was blessed and guarded with rowan tree leaves and the mother's breasts washed with milk. The first nappy was tossed on the front grass with the proper charm being said to ward off witches and a burnt coal was lifted with tongs and tossed through the doorway in case the baby might be stolen.

Means of regaining the child

If, despite these precautions, the child was exchanged a variety of customs could be tried to reclaim the original baby. Many of these involved physical cruelty which today would be punishable by law and can only be accounted for because the perpetrators actually believed that it was a monster they were ousting. A shallow grave was dug on a quarter day (Candlemas, Whitsun, Lammas and Martinmas) and the changeling was buried in it. On returning later it was dug up and the original baby might be found. Another version of this occurred beside the sea when the changeling was buried between high and low tidelines on the shore.

> At dusk the mother was to go to a deep pool in a running stream and toss the spurious baby into the linn. Immediately after the supposed baby disappeared underneath the sombre surface of the water, a harsh scream would follow and the next moment an old man or woman would be seen crawling out of the pool on the other side. The mother on arriving home would find her own baby sound asleep in his cot.
>
> Mythology and Folklore of Lewis, Norman Morrison, 1925

Dropping a burning peat on the changeling often resulted in it disappearing up the chimney and in the morning the original baby was found in its place. Sometimes the mother was advised to go into a wood and leave food and drink beside a fairy knoll while placing the offending creature upon it. If the victuals were removed then the fairies would return her own child.

> A certain woman having put out her child to nurse in the country found when she came to take it home that its form was so much changed that she scarce knew it; nevertheless,

*not knowing what time might do, took it home for her own.
But when, after some years it could neither speak nor go,
the poor woman was fain to carry it, with much trouble in
her arms; and one day, a poor man coming to the door,
"God bless you, mistress," says he, "and your poor child;
be pleased to bestow something on a poor man."*

*"Ah! this child," replied she, "is the cause of all my
sorrow," and related what had happened. . . The old man,
whom age had rendered more prudent in such matters, told
her to out the truth she should make a clear fire, sweep the
hearth very clean, and place the child fast in his chair that
he might not fall before it, and break a dozen eggs and
place four and twenty halfshells before it; then go out, and
listen at the door; for if the child spoke, it was certainly a
changeling; and then she should carry it out, and leave it
on the dunghill to cry, and not to pity it, till she heard its
voice no more. The woman having done all these things
according to these words, heard the child say "Seven years
old was I before I came to the nurse, and four years have
I lived since and never saw so many milkpans before."*

*So the woman took it up, and left it upon the dunghill
to cry and not to be pitied, till at last she thought the voice
went up into the air; and coming, found there her own
natural and well-favoured child.*

Grose's Provincial Glossary

The poisonous flowers of the foxglove were often called
witches' thimbles. They were gathered and boiled then the
liquid put into the mouth of the changeling. The boiled
flowerheads were scattered over its body and it was put into
its cradle wrapped in a blanket and left alone all night in a
barn. In the morning the original baby would be found in the
cradle.

Clearly no-one wanted to accept that their child could be
anything but perfect and any excuse was seized upon avidly.
What happened when there was no improvement does not
seem to feature in the literature.

Modern Days

Many customs still exist and are enacted without any thought as to their origin or meaning. It is still customary in the West of Scotland when people meet a mother with a new baby to drop a silver coin into its pram for luck even if they are not close aquaintances. This stems from the idea that silver brings prosperity not only to the receiver but to the giver. Giving a small gift on the birth of a baby and praising its beauty was tempered by adding, "God bless him", or her to show that no evil was intended.

MARRIAGE

*R*oads were very poor, especially north of the Highland Line, until the nineteenth century. People who lived in towns would rarely venture into the country while those who lived in villages would only occasionally visit nearby villages or the nearest town. In an area where everyone knew each other most young people, and the not so young, selected their marriage partner from a fairly limited number of the opposite sex. Finance and the benefits of acquiring land were as often the reason for a union as falling in love. These considerations played a part in the customs associated with marriage which was very much a community affair and was seen as a great excuse for celebration.

St Bride

Briganta or Brigit was the Celtic goddess of fire, the hearth, healing, marriage, childbirth and of poetry, celebrated by a festival to welcome the spring, usually held on the first day of February. She was renamed Bride and the feast became the Day of Bride. It was thought that she spent the winter imprisoned within Ben Nevis by the Cailleach or Blue Hag who destroyed everything on the earth and brought darkness over the land. On that day Bride was supposed to be rescued by Angus, the ever youthful young god who rode on a white horse. Bride and Angus had the same father, the Dagda, god of fertility and agriculture. Although there were storms Bride eventually chased away the Cailleach who had held sway since Hallowe'en.

Eventually the pagan Bride and St Bride of Kildare became fused and the Day of Bride was sanctified by the Church. From her came the name " bride " for a girl about to be married and all things bridal connected with the ceremony.

Love prophecies

In rural areas the young folk's one aim in life was to get married and have children to help them in their chosen occupation, and from an early age they learned about methods of finding out who their sweetheart would be. Most expected their future spouse to live locally and to have known them most of their life but this did not deter them from carrying out certain customs to pinpoint their future. Some could be carried out at any time, while others had to be observed on specific occasions, such as Hallowe'en, Midsummer and the first of May.

These divinations were taken seriously and great store set by the results. Wishful thinking probably played a part but throught out the ages and in diverse areas the same customs are recorded as having been in vogue. Watered-down versions of many of them still remain, though nowadays they are mostly carried out for fun.

Eggs

Eggs were used in divining, the first-laid egg of a pullet being thought of as giving the best result when combined with fresh spring water. An egg white was dropped into a glass of water then a mouthful taken without swallowing. You then went out for a walk and the first name that you heard spoken would be that of your future spouse.

If egg white was dropped into a glass of water some would sink but some would form shapes. If these shapes were stared at, an object connected with your future spouse's occupation would be seen.

Apples

Apples were another favourite means of divination. One method was to sit in front of a mirror at midnight, alone, cut an apple into nine pieces then, standing with your back to the mirror, point each of the eight pieces towards the left shoulder then eat them, throw the ninth over the left shoulder, turning the head to the left and in the mirror an image of the future husband or wife should appear.

An apple was pared so that the skin came off in one piece. As the clock chimed twelve the pared skin was swung three times around the head without breaking it. It was then flung over the left shoulder and on landing would form the first letter of the intended's name. If it broke there would not be a wedding that year. Or if the paring was set above the lintel of the door the first person to enter would have the same Christian name as a future spouse. This custom was also described by Robert Burns in the poem *Hallowe'en*, using the stalks of oats rather than the apple skin.

Nuts

Nuts were also thought to have magic powers and it was common to burn them in the fire. Two were chosen to represent a lad and lass and if they burned quietly together all would be well but if they spit and burst true love would be anything but smooth.

Who will he be?

In the fishing communities around the Ayrshire coast the girls threw herring fat at a wall. If it slid down slowly in a straight line their future husband would be upright, if it slid down unevenly the husband would be crooked.

On Midsummer's Eve a girl picked the stonecrop or Midsummer Men. (*sedum telephium*) and held it above her head. If it bent to the right her lover was true but if it veered to the left he was false. Another Midsummer's Eve practice was for a girl to run three times around the churchyard sunwise scattering hempseed and saying:

> *Hempseed I sow,*
> *let hempseed grow.*
> *He that will my sweetheart be,*
> *Come after me now.*
>
> Traditional

If she looked behind she would see her future husband copying her actions.

A further custom which was carried on out of doors was dipping the sark sleeve. A girl went to where a stream flowed south and dipped the sleeve of a shirt into the water. She took it home to dry and lay in bed watching it in the firelight. The wraith of her lover would appear to turn the sleeve.

> *The last Hallowe'en I was waukin*
> *My droukit sark-sleeve, as ye ken,*
> *His likeness came up the house staukin,*
> *And the very grey breeks o' Tam Glen.*
>
> Tam Glen, Robert Burns, 1789

Who will she be?

Men had their own customs. Three coggies or bowls were filled, one with clear water, one with water and soot, and one left empty. The lad was blindfolded and the bowls turned round. He chose one. If the water in it was clear his bride would be a maiden, if sooty a widow and if empty he would remain a bachelor. In the Highlands a man had to slip off unnoticed to a field which had been ploughed. He had to enter it from the western side, ensuring that the furrows ran north to south. He had to cross eleven ridges to stand in the centre of the twelfth, and listen intently. If he heard sobs or shrieks this foretold an early death, if music and dancing it indicated that he would soon marry.

Dreams

Dreams ,often interpreted to suit the dreamer, were supposed to reveal the future and appear in the selection of a mate in several customs. For example if a girl picked a root which grew beneath the mugwort plant, placed it under her pillow and slept on it she would dream of her future husband. Brides cake or bannock was another prized item to dream on, as was the christening piece given to the first person to meet the child going to its baptism. When sleeping in a strange bed if a ring was put on a finger and a shoe placed below the bed, which then had to be got into backwards, the loved one would appear in a dream.

Omens

There were other omens. If new shoes were laid on a table it foretold a marriage, or if the marriage shaek, a noise like the ticking of a watch, was heard there would soon be a bride in the family.

Valentine's Day

Valentine's Day has always been celebrated as a time for lovers to reveal their secret love. A more certain way of finding a partner was the custom of Valentine Dealing. This took place on February the fourteenth. An equal number of male and female names were written on pieces of paper which were placed in separate hats. These were carried round the company and each person drew a name from the appropriate hat. Whichever names were paired the two became sweethearts for the following year and gifts were exchanged.

> Yestreen at the Valentine dealing,
> My heart to me mou gied a sten;
> For thrice I drew ane without failing,
> And thrice it was written "Tam Glen".
> Tam Glen, Robert Burns, 1789

The modern custom of sending cards was developed in the Victorian era and anonymous greetings with verses urging the postman to deliver quickly to "my valentine" stems from these. "Postman, postman, do not tarry, take this to the one

I'll marry" or "Postman, postman, do your duty, take this to my fair haired beauty". Across the seal of the envelope the letters SWALK means "sealed with a loving kiss".

Courtship

Courtship and marriage had in both rural and urban areas many customs attached, from ways of foretelling who will marry whom to all sorts of things which had to be done to ensure every chance of a good marriage. If, even by chance, some well-known custom were omitted and tragedy or disharmony should occur within the first year this would be pounced on as the reason. A great sense of community involvement in matters amorous abounded to prevent such omissions with friends and neighbours giving advice and organising each step of the way to give the couple's romance every chance of being successful. In many ways, especially in rural areas, social life was limited and any excuse for fun and enjoyment was welcomed.

Winching

There were few opportunities to meet members of the opposite sex, especially in remote areas. One such was the Feeing Fairs, held in most towns to allow farmhands and domestic servants to be hired for a six-month period, which were favourite places for young men to size up and flirt with the fair sex. They often presented fairings such as coloured ribbons or sweetmeats to the girl they fancied. The girls enjoyed the excitement of consulting the spaewife or fortune teller waiting to have her hand crossed with silver to predict health, wealth and happiness and to describe a future suitor. Sometimes at such fairs there were horse races after which the winner would place a bonnet on the head of his chosen one.

Walking out

In towns walking out was a popular activity and young men and girls would parade up and down streets or parks or the seaside. Gradually they would pair off and were said to be eind, in modern parlance – an item. When the lovers agreed to become betrothed they stood on opposite banks of a burn and, dipping their fingers in the water, joined hands across it and exchanged vows. Others licked the thumbs of their right hand and pressed them tightly together as a bond.

In rural areas, however, the would-be suitor had often to tramp many miles after his day's work to visit his loved one. They would meet beside bushes or trees or among the barley rigs.

Rocking

The Rocking was a popular event where girls from neighbouring farms gathered in a farm kitchen. The ostensible reason was for the girls and older women to spin lint on their distaffs or rocks but later in the evening when the men arrived the occasion generally ended up as a party.

> On Fastern'een we had a rockin'
> Ta ca' the crack and weave our stockin';
> And there was muckle fun and jokin',
> Ye needna doubt;
> At length we had a hearty yokin'
> At sang about.
>
> Epistle to J. Lapraik, Robert Burns, 1785

Watching the fold

In July at the ewe-buchts, where the sheep were milked, or watching the fold so that lambs who had been weaned did not return to their mothers, was a grand excuse for lad and lass to pass the entire night together.

> My Peggie is a young thing,
> Just entered in her teens
> Fair as the day and sweet as May,
> Fair as the day, and always gay:
> My Peggie is a young thing
> And I'm nae very auld,

And weel I like to meet her
At the waukin' o' the fauld.

The Gentle Shepherd,
Allan Ramsay, 1729

The lads often wore a sprig of scented wormwood, commonly known as Lad's Love, in their lapel to show that they had found a sweatheart.

Other occasions for merriment and pairing off were at the sheep-shearing, the Kirn or harvest celebrations and at Hallowe'en.

Feast days

Holy Fairs, or Sacramental Fast Days, when communion was served to members of the Church of Scotland in the open air, were an excellent excuse to meet and pair off. Sometimes these lasted for almost a week and folk travelled long distances to attend.

The lads an' lasses blythely bent
To mind baith saul an' body,
Sit round the table weel content,
An' steer about the toddy:
On this ane's dress, an' that ane's leuk,
They're makin observations;
While some are cozie i' the neuk,
An' forming assignations
To meet some day.

The Holy Fair, Robert Burns, 1785

The Thursday preceeding the communion Sundays was, in spring and autumn, a holy day when preparatory services were held and all shops were closed. This custom remains in the May and September weekend holidays which still are taken in most Scottish towns.

Bundling

Bundling was a custom mentioned in several areas but it seems to have lasted longest in Orkney. It encouraged a lad and lass to share a bed but they did so fully clothed and with the girl's legs firmly tied into a bolster cover, or in some areas the bolster, a long double pillow, was placed down the centre of the bed and they lay on either side of it. Thus during long winter's nights the couple talked and got to know one another better with the blessing of her family.

Holidays

Young lovers often carved their entwined initials on the trunk of a tree or sometimes into stone. These were known as marriage or bridal stones and some still exist. In urban areas young people met at the common green and at fair time and New Year when the mills and factories closed for a holiday at the shows with their stalls and joyrides.

In the twentieth century dance halls became popular and had their own unwritten customs. The men stood on one side of the floor between dances and the girls on the other. As each dance was announced – "Please take your partners for –" there would be a mad dash across the floor to choose a girl. The boy posed the legendary question, "Are ye dancin?" the reply being, "Are ye askin'?" Generally a different partner was chosen for each dance until by mutual agreement there came the offer to lumber the girl home. This meant accompanying her either on foot, bus or tramcar to where she lived in the hope of a cuddle and a goodnight kiss. Many lads missed their last tram and had a long walk home, while some were fly and found out the destination before they committed themselves to a girl in the first place.

Betrothal

The next step after the courtship was the betrothal. It was, however, customary for the lad to ask the father of the bride for her hand and to discuss with him his prospects and if he had the means to keep her. If the father approved he gave his permission to approach his daughter.

Sometimes when the lad asked his lassie if she would marry him, he hinted that she was not the only one in contention.

I've nine milk ewes, my Marion,
A cow and a brawny quey;
I'll gie them a' to my Marion,
Just on her bridal day.

I'm young and stout, my Marion;
Nane dances like me on the green:
And gin ye forsake me, Marion,
I'll e'en gae draw up wi' Jean.

Tea-Table Miscellany,
Allan Ramsay, 1724

The bride was expected to have a bottom drawer, a collection of bed-linen, blankets, table linen and furnishing for the bedroom, which her kinfolk would help her to gather together.

Her father might also give her some cattle and sheep or a dowry of money. In the sixteenth century it was not uncommon for lairds to go into debt to provide a dowry for their daughters. The following cynical poem suggests that money can buy love or at least a husband.

Be a lassie e'er sae black,
Gin she hae the penny siller,
Set her upon Tintock tap,
The wind will blaw a man till her.

Be a lassie e'er sae fair,
An' she want the penny siller,
A flee may fell her in the air,
Before a man be evened till her.

Traditional

Rèitach

In the Western Isles a reitach, or formal asking, was a complicated affair which usually took place after it was tacitly known that a young couple were contemplating marriage.

There was a gathering of friends at the bride's home, one of whom had been appointed to ask the bride's father in the bridegroom-to-be's stead. It was a sort of game, with never a direct reference to the matter in hand. The talk would be of other things until the friend said that he had heard there was a ewe lamb, or a boat that was needing looked after and he would be glad to arrange for this to happen. The father would agree and say that he knew it would be in safe hands.

Afterwards there was a party which might go on until the wee small hours. The mother and other relatives and neighbours contributed items of food; broth, chickens and potatoes. There would be a sit-down meal. Miraculously the fiddler and accordionist would be present as well as the best maids and bestman-to-be, although everyone pretended that it was a great surprise. On Barra the custom, slightly changed in character, is still in existence.

Speerin' bottle

In Shetland the young hopeful arrived at the door of his intended. He was invited in and shyly placed a small parcel on the box bed. He approached the family and shook hands with them all in turn, ignoring his prospective bride and the hints given by her relations that they know why he has called. Eventually her father would make an excuse to go out. The suitor had to follow and ask him for his daughter's hand in marriage. When it was agreed they returned and the parcel was opened to reveal the speerin' bottle which was handed round for a toast. It would, of course, contain whisky.

Washing the feet

Another ceremony, a remnant of Druidical purification rites and symbolic of a fresh start in life, was washing the feet of the bride and groom-to-be which seems to have taken place in some areas in their separate homes and in others at the home of the bride immediately after the betrothal. The bridegroom and bride having stripped off their shoes and stockings, the guests smeared their feet and legs with oil or grease, which they next rubbed over with soot. Then they used soap and coal cinders. The victims did not resist too heartily and there was a great deal of laughter and teasing. The rest of the night was given over to song and dance helped on by glasses of whisky.

Other reports place this ceremony in the home of the bride on the eve of the wedding. It was a much tamer affair with only girls and women present. A wedding ring was thrown into a basin of water placed on the floor and there was a scramble by the unmarried girls to find it. The first to do so would be the next bride. More recently friends put on the bride-to-be's engagement ring on the third finger of their left hand, turned it three times towards their heart and made a wish.

Leap year

Leap year gave the lassies a chance to propose. If the chosen suitor refused he had to buy the lady a new dress or a pair of kid gloves. A betrothal was as legally binding as a marriage so if a breach of promise occurred, when an engagement or betrothal was broken, the girl could sue in court for recompense.

Prenuptials

Many decisions had to be made and customs observed as soon as the couple had become engaged. The day and date of the wedding required thought. It was considered unlucky to wed during a waning moon, in the months of January or May and on certain days of the week. Friday, which was also called Venusday, was dedicated to Freya, the Norse goddess of love and was popular for weddings.

The banns had to be proclaimed in church for three Sundays. This was a notification to the congregation of the couples intention to marry and anyone who had a legitimate objection could stop the ceremony taking place. It was the duty of the bestman to cry them, that is to give the session clerk of the parish the information which allowed him to make out the proclamation.

Cryin' siller

The money paid to the Kirk for calling the banns was known as cryin' siller, The word wed means pledge, so those wishing to marry had to leave a pledge or a pawn, either money or clothing which was forfeited if a penny wedding, with music and dancing, took place as the Church disapproved of it. If the event was called off the pawn went into the poor-box. In some fishing communities it was a pledge against wild behaviour.

Wedding presents

Bridals were considered community property and it was important that everyone had the opportunity to take part. Neighbours and parents of friends gave wee mindings or small gifts. In the Highlands hand-crafted wooden or wickerwork items such as cogs, horn spoons and tongs were often specially made.

Show of presents

A traditional custom, especially in the West of Scotland, was the show of presents which, while it has changed a great deal is still taking place. Originally it was a way of thanking female neighbours and friends for their gifts by putting them on display. It was held in the bride's home for two days, both afternoon and evening, when a wide selection of home baking was served along with sandwiches and tea. It was a good way of letting the two families meet when the betrothed pair did not live in the same community. Nowadays shows are normally held at weekends, men often attend and more sophisticated fare is served.

In all villages in Moray the bride and bridegroom invited their guests to a "bucking" the night before the wedding when supper was served and the presents displayed.

Bestman and bridesmaids

The appointment of a bestman was a throwback to the days of raiding parties when maidens were abducted and forced to marry. They also acted as defenders if the girl's family came after her and tried to snatch her back. The selection of a bestman and two bridesmaids was made from friends or family and they had several tasks to carry out. The bridesmaids went round issuing invitations, one to the bride's friends, the other to the groom's, while the bride and groom traditionally invited relations and close friends themselves.

Tarred and feathered

One of the bestman's tasks was to organise the fun and games on the eve of the wedding. In Stonehaven the bridegroom was tarred and feathered, in Kingussie blackened with soot and flour or sometimes boot-polish or cocoa was used, anything which made a mess. In more recent times lipstick was popular but it was very hard to remove and many a red-faced bridegroom appeared in the kirk. Another ploy was to remove the bridegroom's trousers and tie him to a lamppost or tie him up, put him on a bus and give the conductor some money asking him to allow the victim to travel up and down to the terminus for as long as the fare was covered.

Referred to as stag nights, these now take place a few nights earlier to allow the participants to recover and are purely drinking sessions with sometimes kiss-o-grams or strip-o-grams appearing, occasionally dressed as police and threatening arrest.

Pay-off

The bride did not escape the ribbing. Mostly she was placed in embarrassing positions but sometimes she too was "blackened"

"Oh they make a right mess o ye! They would plan to get hold of the bride either comin from her work or whatever she was doin, and get a hold of the groom in the same way. Just sort o trap them intae something so you could get a

hold of them and really make a mess of them. . . tar,
syrup, treacle, feathers, chocolate."

Elizabeth Stewart, Mintlaw, 1988

More usually the bride was dressed up by her workmates, especially in factories and mills, although in towns office workers found themselves with a coat outside-in and covered with paper flowers, a lace curtain on their heads and expected to type sitting on a chanty, a chamberpot filled with salt. The bride carried the chanty when she was taken through the town or village, usually in a barrow or nowadays on a supermarket trolley, for her pay-off. Everyone who contributed money claimed a kiss from the bride and took a lick of salt from the chanty for luck. In Ayrshire these customs are very much alive. The bride, in Kilmarnock, being referred to as the bosola has to jump the chanty three times for luck. Originally the women and girls walked to the home of the bride for a feast but nowadays the bride is taken into pubs and the party end up in high spirits having taken a sip from the penny-pint, offered for a symbolical payment, in each hostelry. It was also a custom in fishing villages for the bride to jump the creels for luck or be led in farming areas to be led three times sunwise round the shepherd's crook.

Hen night

A gathering of womenfolk for a night out before the wedding, called a hen night, comes from the old custom of the women congregating at the home of the bride to pluck hens which would be prepared for the wedding feast.

Salt

In rural areas the evening before the wedding the bridesmaid carried the bride's chanty filled with salt to her new home and sprinkled some on the floor for luck. The tocher or bride's goods were also taken and the bridal bed made up. Sometimes other presents were taken and put into place. It was very bad luck if the bride should trip on entering her new home or break a dish.

Weddings

There was a variety of weddings. Free weddings were held when the bride's father paid for all the food and drink, while penny weddings implied that each guest should contribute a sum of money to defray expenses for food, drink and the fiddler. Any spare money left over was given to the young couple to help them to set up their home. A dinner wedding was when close family and friends were invited to eat the wedding dinner provided by the bride's father. This was sometimes followed by dancing and the arrival of more guests. Contrary to English custom, a Scots wedding always continued into the evening. However nowadays the economic cost has risen so high that there is often a division between full guests, who attend the ceremony the reception and dinner, and evening guests who join in later for the dancing. In the 1920s and 1930s afternoon weddings took place in hotels but were never popular with guests since there was a strict rule that no dancing could take place at the reception. Sometimes the bridal party would go on to the theatre.

Penny weddings

Attempts to ban this type of wedding were made by the General Assembly of the Church of Scotland several times during the seventeenth and eighteenth centuries because it considered such weddings led to promiscuous dancing. It tried to fine members £20 Scots and to rebuke them in front of the congregation but the people took little heed and "scandalous occasions" are described as having taken place in Haddington and Dunbar in 1647.

> Multitudes exceeding twenty assembled on these occasions.
> The paying of extravagant sums exceeding 12/- Scots for a
> man and 8/- Scots for a woman caused great immoralities
> – piping and dancing before and after dinner or supper,
> drinking after dinner. . . "Moreover, loose speeches,
> singing of licentious songs, and profane minstrelling, in

> *time of dinner or supper tends to great deboshry. Through*
> *all which causes penny bridals, in our judgement, become*
> *seminaries of all profanation."*
>
> Domestic Annals of Scotland, Vol 2, From the Reformation
> to the Revolution, Robert Chambers, n.d.

Alternative forms of marriage

Other forms of co-habitation were known. In Scotland there is a custom which allows a woman to be declared a common-law wife, which means that a couple recognised by friends and neighbours as such for a number of years can, by habit and repute, have the same rights of inheritance as a legally married couple.

Trial marriages took place to ensure that an heir would be born, known as handfasting. A simple declaration made before a witness, often at the annual fair, bound a couple hand in fist for a year and a day, for which time they agreed to live together. If they were happy with the arrangement they could marry when the "book in the busum" priest came to the next fair. He might marry several couples on the same day. If the couple separate, however, and a child was conceived or born it was the responsibility of the father to care for it. This child was treated as legitimate and had equal standing with brothers and sisters of a formal marriage.

No stigma was attached to the woman who was free to find a new mate. Handfasting was outlawed by the 1939 Marriage (Scotland) Act.

Owre-boggie weddings

> *There is some sweetness, I should think, and gallantry felt*
> *in weddings of this kind; there is something glorious in a*
> *trip to Gretna Green with a lovely lady. . . Those who plot*
> *in secret are called "owre-boggie fowk"; and displaced*
> *priests, who used to bind people contrary to canon laws. . .*
> *were designated "auld boggies".*
>
> Scottish Gallovidian Encyclopedia, John Mactaggart, 1824

These appealed to runaways from England and Wales who wished to marry and avail themselves of the different laws north of the border where the legal age for marriage was sixteen as opposed then to twenty-one in the south. Gretna Green became famous as a place for runaways to wed, being just over the border into Scotland, although couples could be married over the iron, as these marriages were termed, anywhere in the country. Blacksmiths allowed this ceremony to be carried out over the anvil as it was considered lucky. Two witnesses were all that was required. Occasionally an auld boggie priest would officiate. The practice became more difficult in 1856 when it was made a condition that either the bride or bridegroom-to-be had to be resident in Scotland for three weeks before the marriage.

Location

Weddings can take place in the home of the bride, in the manse, in a hotel, even on board a boat so long as it is tied up at the quay. In Scotland it is the minister who carries out the sacrament who is licensed and not the location.

Fisherfolk

At Collieston, Aberdeenshire after the church service a feast was provided for the whole community who then moved to Forvie Sands where the bride and groom led off the dancing of the "Lang Reel o' Collieston" in which everybody took part.

It was customary when a member of a fishing boat crew married to dress the boat all over with flags. Money was given to the crew to buy whisky to celebrate the occasion. In Aberdeenshire the youngest member of the crew carried a flag to the house of the bride where he wrapped it around her and was rewarded with a kiss.

Dress and deportment

The formal wedding gown was not adopted by ordinary folk until the twentieth century. Girls before then wore their best frock or had a new one made for the occasion. When trying on her wedding dress a stitch was left undone and she never made her dress entirely on her own. The colour white was introduced by Queen Victoria; before this most colours except green, unlucky because it was the choice of the fairies, and black because it was worn for mourning, were chosen. The rich often chose silver while blue meant constancy: "marry in blue, love ever true."

When the bride was bathed she dressed throughout in new garments if possible and put on a garter, sometimes of blue ribbon and lace. The old custom of "Something old, something new, something borrowed, something blue" is still very much adhered to. She should have a silver coin in her left shoe and be careful to put her right shoe on first to avoid bad luck. She should never look in a mirror fully dressed for her wedding. Her veil is usually worn over her face until the couple are pronounced husband and wife.

The bridegroom was not left out in the sartorial stakes. He often wore buckled shoes, if possible with silver buckles and sometimes an embroidered waistcoat. He might buy a new wedding coat, which might have to last him all his life and serve for going to the kirk, christenings, weddings, burials and all other special occasions. It was considered lucky for the groom if someone slipped salt into his pocket unseen.

Having duly got dressed both bride and groom had to have all knots about their person removed before the ceremony to ensure that there would be no barrier to fertility. As soon as the ceremony was over they were retied; thus being married is also known as tying the knot.

Scramble

On departing from her home the bride threw the marriage ba' which was a type of football gaily decorated and sought after by the young men. Later only the name remained and money to buy a ball was thrown instead. Thus the scramble or scoor oot, scatter or poor-oot began. The bridegroom also threw money on leaving home and children would vie with each other to retrieve the coins. It is still common for workers along the route of the bridal car, usually while it is travelling to the reception, to shout "hard up, kick the can," as it passes by. In some areas the boys and girls of the neighbourhood assembled in front of the bride's house calling out

> Bell money, bell money, shabby waddin', shabby waddin', canna spare a bawbee.

Setting out

At Avoch, a fishing village on the Black Isle it was customary to marry young. The celebrations took place on a Friday, a lucky day for weddings but not for much else, and continued throughout the weekend. To ward off witches or evil influences the following custom was carried out.

> When the bridegroom's party arrives at the church door, the bestman unties the shoe upon the left foot of the bridegroom, and forms a cross with a nail or knife upon the right side of the door. The shoe, of course, remains untied until next morning.
>
> Rev. James Gibson, 1895

If the wedding was in the kirk, the bride's party set out led by her father. Although sometimes the bridegroom sent two young men called sens to escort the bride to church to ensure that she would not be abducted. They had to avoid meeting a funeral on the way to the wedding. The bride had to approach the church from right to left and sometimes she walked three times around the church sunwise before entering.

The bridegroom arrived with the bridesmaids and his father, preceded by a piper, and was escorted to the bridesteel or pew reserved for him and his bestman to await the arrival of the bride. She was met at the door by the church officer and walked up the aisle on the arm of a brother or other male relative to stand to the right of her groom. It was customary, however, for widows to choose a matron of honour to fulfil this task. The giving away of the bride by her father is a more recent custom.

Rings

The ring, symbolic of a pledge, dates back to Roman times. The custom of placing the ring on the third finger of the bride's left hand was banned after the Reformation by Presbyterians as it was considered to be a popish relic. It became fashionable again in 1660 after the Restoration. Often the same ring was used as engagement and wedding ring and was worn on the right hand and transferred to the left hand on marriage. Men rarely wore engagement or wedding rings, their appearance being fairly recent, especially the inclusion of an exchange of rings as part of the wedding ceremony.

Celebration

There was a rush to kiss the bride, the winner often being the minister. Pistols could be fired and church bells rung, not just in celebration but to keep away evil spirits. Depending on the man's occupation, the couple sometimes passed under an arch of appropriate items as they left the church, such as sickles, boat hooks or swords. The same custom can still be seen today in the form of a guard of honour.

Running the Broose

A now obsolete custom which was very popular was that of running the broose or braize, which originated in the days when there was a possibility of the bride being abducted. The mothers of the bride and groom did not attend the ceremony but waited at the couple's new home. The young men raced to be the first to arrive with the information that all was well and to claim the award of a bottle of whisky.

Confetti

On leaving the church rice, confetti or rose petals were thrown over the couple as a symbol of fertility. A shoe was thrown after the couple by the bride's father as a symbol of the transfer of responsibility for her from him to her husband.

Unloosing the bride's garter

> *The next ceremony was the garter, which the bridegroom's man attempted to pull from her leg; but shedropt it throw her petticot on the floor. This was white and silver ribbon, which was cut in small morsels* [and given] *to everyone in the company.*
>
> Caldwell papers, Elizabeth Mure, 1750

The reception

The reception was held either at the home of the bride, in the village hall or in a barn and later hotels grew in popularity. By tradition the minister in Church of Scotland weddings acted as master of ceremonies, making a speech in which he told anecdotes or jokes, and introduced the other speakers. He usually proposed the first toast to the happy pair.

> *The bridal-day it came to pass,*
> *With mony a blithesome lad and lass:*
> *But siccan a day there never was,*
> *Sic mirth was never seen.*
> *The winsome couple straiket hands,*
> *Mess John tied up the marriage bands.*
> *Sic hirdum-dirdum and sic din,*
> *Wi' he o'er her ,an' she o'er him;*
> *The minstrels they did never blin'*
> *Wi' muckle mirth and glee;*
> *And aye they bobbit, and aye they beck't,*
> *And aye they reeled, and aye they set.*
>
> Muirland Wullie, traditional ballad

Wedding cake

After the formal meal the bride's mother used to break a bannock or bridescake (a type of shortbread) over the head of the bride. If it broke into small pieces this meant that the marriage would be fruitful but if it remained in large lumps it boded ill and could signify infertility. The cake often had trinkets such as thimbles hidden in it. Unmarried girls scrambled to get a piece so that they could put it under their pillow to dream on. This developed into the wedding cake made with fruit and decorated with marzipan and icing, which grew larger and had several tiers, the top tier traditionally being kept for the christening of the first child. The cake was cut by the bride alone and not by both the bride and groom as is more usual today. Pieces of cake were handed round at the wedding and were given to everyone who gave a present to the couple. Sometimes young girls crumbled a piece of cake through a wedding ring to ensure that they would marry. The bride's cog, or bowl, was passed around from lip to lip filled with hot ale, whisky, cream, beaten eggs, sugar and spices and everyone drank her health.

Favours

[The giving of favours, a small keepsake, to the guests is thought of as originating in Italy, however the custom is recorded in Scotland in the eighteenth century.] *The bride's favours are sewn on her gown from top to bottom, and round the neck and sleeves. The moment the wedding ceremony was performed the whole company ran to her and pulled off the favours; in an instant she was stripped of all of them. The bride's mother then came in with a basket of favours belonging to the bridegroom; those and the bride's were the same, with the livery's of their families, hers pink and white, his gold and blue colour. All the company dined and supped together and had a ball in the evening.*

Caldwell Papers, Elizabeth Mure, 1750

Dancing

By tradition the first dance was danced by the bride and groom. After one turn of the floor the bestman and the chief

bridesmaid, the bride's mother and the groom's father
followed by the bride's father and the groom's mother take the
floor. In Galloway if the bride is the younger and has an older
unmarried sister she had to dance barefoot and in other areas
she gave the bride green garters.

O! how can I be blythe and gay,
Whan this is Mallie's wadding day,
For I should first ha ,e been away,
O! she has beat me clean,
Alas, puir me, what will I do,
This day maun dance withoot a shoe,
Maun thole the scorn o' a' fowk too,
And lie my lane ate, een o.
    Mallie's Wadding Day, traditional ballad

Music was usually provided by a fiddler and accordionist who
played reels, strathspeys and hornpipes. The Lancers, the
Dashing White Sergeant and the wild Strip the Willow were
often danced. At the beginning and end of each dance a kiss
could be claimed, although kissing games such as Babbity
Bowster were also played.

Wha learned you to dance,
Babbity Bowster, Babbity Bowster?
Wha learned you to dance,
Babbity Bowster, brawly.
My minny learned me to dance,
Babbity Bowster, Babbity Bowster?
My minny learned me to dance,
Babbity Bowster, brawly.
    Traditional

The marriage guests joined hands, male and female alternately
forming a circle which revolved round one guest who held a
white hankie or a bolster to be placed on the ground in front of
the chosen one who then knelt on it and bestowed a kiss. That
person then took their place in the centre and so it went on.

At the end of the evening the Grand March was performed involving the whole company. This was followed by "Auld Lang Syne" and sometimes the bridal party were pushed into the centre of the ring and "For they are jolly good fellows" was sung. In the days of penny weddings anyone attending and not contributing was called a whistlebinkie, although if they brought a penny whistle, told stories or sang to entertain the company they might be forgiven. In some areas the groom went round the company with a plate for donations.

Post-nuptials

Several ceremonies used to take place after the wedding. In Barra the two mothers sprinkled water on the marriage bed and blessed it. In Mull the young couple had to sleep in the barn on their first night and in Lewis they lived for a week with the bride's parents before going to their own home.

When the couple arrived at their new home the bridegroom carried the bride over the threshold as it would be unlucky if she tripped. The mothers put the keys of the house into her hands and she was given the fire tongs and had to place a peat on the fire.

At one time the beddin' o' the bride was conducted with great enthusiasm. The men stayed outside while the womenfolk undressed the bride and put on her night attire, ensuring that no knots were tied. The bridegroom then entered and undressed. As the bride sat up in bed all the men came in and claimed a kiss. The bride then threw her left stocking, which was known in Galloway as throwin' the hosen, and whoever it hit would be next to marry. Willow was placed beneath the bed as a symbol of fertility.

The women the next morning would roll the bride's hair on wooden bodkins and cover it with a curtch, which was a fine piece of linen doubled diagonally and passed round the head close to the forehead. Young women fastened the ends behind while old ones fastened them under the chin.

Creeling the bridegroom

Sometimes the bridegroom had a creel filled with stones put on his back with the band around his head. As he staggered beneath the weight his friends kept adding to it. Eventually the bride was handed a knife to cut him free, to cheers. This symbolised the sharing of life's burdens together. Another form of creeling took place in Ayrshire. The young men carried the creel in turn through the streets, allowing themselves to be caught and kissed by the young women until the creel was put back on to the shoulders of the bridegroom when, as before, his new bride rescued him. In Berwick once a year all the newly married men were creeled, carrying the creel from one house to that of the next married neighbour.

On his return to work the bridegroom had to pay off his workmates by standing his hand for beer. If he did not he was rubbed all over with dust and grime which in mining villages in Fife, was also called creeling.

So many customs old and new, some obsolete yet many still existing in one form or another to ensure that the newly wedded pair will have every chance of happiness and success.

DEATH

*D*eath was the ultimate journey and was treated with respect. To the Celtic peoples the veil between this world and the next was very fine and they lived their lives ever conscious of that other world. The spirit was vulnerable from the moment of death and needed to be guarded against the forces of evil until it safely crossed over the bridge between life and eternity.

The Picts in the Bronze Age placed the dead bodies in stone-lined cists and buried these underground, usually with a cup containing wine. Later food was added and the spot marked with a cup and ring stone. Still later the remains were cremated and buried in urns underground.

Christianity continued these rites of passage and the Catholic Church incorporated or at least tolerated the old customs and even after the Reformation many of them survived. Sometimes the General Assembly of the Church of Scotland attempted to ban certain rituals because it believed that there was too much drinking and jollity instead of solemn behaviour. In 1645 it banned attendance at wakes but the ruling was largely ignored.

Modern attitudes to death and the treatment of the corpse would have been frowned on as late as the 1950s, although undertakers were employed from around 1820 by the better off. Most families accepted that the corpse of their relative should lie in the house for at least three days so that respects could be paid. The modern idea that it be moved immediately to a chapel of rest would have been seen as acting with indecent haste and preventing the normal customs from being carried out. The custom now adopted of bringing the hearse already loaded with coffin and flowers to the front door where the family enter the funeral limousines to follow it to the cemetery or crematorium, or even in some cases meet it at the gate of the resting place would astonish folk brought up to observe the old traditions.

However it is the ever-changing tradition, a seeming contradiction in terms, which can come full circle. In Biblical times it was believed that the dead envied the living especially if the corpse was young or middle-aged and that burial should take place as quickly as possible, for the corpse would be seeking a companion. In the Middle Ages in Scotland all customs were to prevent the ghost or spirit of the corpse returning to haunt the living. All the rites performed then were to protect those still alive against the envy of the dead. The same customs have gradually moved through being performed to ward off evil spirits during the belief in the supernatural uppermost in the seventeenth and eighteenth centuries, towards today being carried out as a mark of respect for the dead and sorrow for the living to whom the corpse meant most.

Sometimes today a service is held either in the chapel of rest at the undertaker's or in the church where the deceased was a member of the congregation and the cortege leaves from there. Catholics still permit the coffin to lie overnight in the church. A mass is heard on the evening previous to the funeral after the mourners have walked behind the hearse from the home of the deceased.

The modern funeral does follow much the same form as those of the past. The service, the committal and a gathering for refreshments, although now this is at a hotel as often as it is at the home of the deceased.

It is possible nowadays to have a secular funeral with no religious trappings. Often this is at a crematorium and friends make all the arrangements and carry out the service which may include a eulogy by a friend and the deceased's favourite songs may be played. Many people without any religious belief feel that it is less hypocritical to have such a funeral than a "Christian" one.

Omens

When few people ventured far from their birthplace and the immediate community was their whole knowledge of the world, they were inevitably strongly influenced by the beliefs and ideas of that community and under great pressure to conform at all times. The belief that the hand of fate was present at every event led to an acceptance of ideas which, viewed from later centuries, seem naive and unrealistic.

In past centuries, especially the seventeenth and eighteenth, fear of the power of the devil was uppermost in the minds of Scots and belief in the evil eye and in witchcraft was widespread not only among ordinary people but also among priests and ministers. King James VI of Scotland wrote a treatise against witchcraft and kirk sessions punished members for trafficking with Satan until the end of the eighteenth century.

Friths and omens, the meaning of which were orally handed down through the ages, could determine the outcome of an illness, and observers felt that many a boiled ham, traditional fare at a funeral, was prepared on the strength of these. Many people believed that signs were given when someone was about to die to allow them time to prepare themselves and make their peace. These beliefs were not confined to simple minds but were held by all walks of society.

If the patient should make, to those watching, a miraculous recovery, the omens seem to have been discounted, but if death occurred the gossips read meanings into every action that took place in the period leading up to it and interpreted these to suit their own ideas. Infectious diseases were not understood and the old custom of sitting with the sick in a stuffy room led to the spread of fevers, especially during outbreaks of cholera; these diseases were seen as God exercising his judgement and bringing his wrath to bear on the community.

> *A Yule wi'out snaws,*
> *A Januar' wi' haws,*
> *Bring the deid-thraws*
> > Witchwood, John Buchan, 1922

If a mouse squeaked behind a bed, if a raven flew over the house or a cock crowed at midnight death was imminent. If someone's ears were ringing then news of a death would come soon. Sparrows hovering around a house indicated the death of a child, while three meadow-pipits singing near a house was a requiem for a child.

Leaving the door of the dead-room slightly open was another custom carried out in the belief that if foul play had taken place the corpse would speak the name of the perpetrator. This was a common theme of the traditional ballads.

The deid-drap which could be the sound of a drop of water falling solidly on the ground, hearing strange knocking sounds or having a coal in the shape of a coffin jump from the fire to the hearth was feared as a precursor of death. These signs were accepted as fact and no attempt was made to find another interpretation.

Dogs

Dogs were believed to have an uncanny sense of the moment of death and if a pet dog refused to approach an invalid that was taken as a sign that the end was near. If a dog barked three times it was a warning of death and to prevent it a stone should be thrown on the first bark.

> *In one week died Lady Kilbirnie and her husband of a*
> *pestilential fever. . . In the day of sickening of the laird*
> *and lady, his dogs went into the close, and an unco dog*
> *coming among them, they all set up a barking, with their*
> *faces up to heaven, howling, yelling, and youphing ; and*

when the laird called to them they would not come to him
as in former times.

Domestic Annals of Scotland, Vol 2, From the Reformation
to the Revolution, Robert Chambers, n.d.

Deid thraws

A torn sheet showed signs of struggle and was believed to indicate a violent death and if the patient was in the deid-thraws but was dying slowly this indicated that a charm or the evil eye had been put upon them, and every lock in the house must be opened so that the spirit could escape.

Corpse-lights

Others maintained that nature exhibited her own warnings. Deid-lights were seen hanging around in a wood. These probably came from phosphorated hydrogen hovering above decaying matter but they were thought to presage a death. They were also considered to be an indication of the whereabouts of the victim of foul play.

Leave aff yer doukin on the day,
And douk upon the night;
And where the sackles knight lies slain,
The candles will burn bright.

Traditonal ballad

Trial by touch

The maiden touch'd the clay-cauld corpse,
A drap it never bled;
The Ladye laid her hand on him
And soon the ground was red.

The Ballad of Earl Richard, traditional ballad

This refers to the custom of trial by touch where foul play was suspected. If the person who committed the deed touched the corpse it was seen to bleed. The fact that moving a corpse can produce blood at the nose or mouth did not seem to be considered.

Meeting with a funeral

In the Borders a man unexpectedly meeting a funeral procession had to take off his hat and turn and walk part of the way with it or he might die soon. If the bearers are carrying the coffin he must take his turn for a short distance. Then he should bow to the mourners and proceed on his original way.

Money

Money had an important role in death. In the nineteenth and early twentieth centuries, in Lewis, boys were paid sixpence to run round and inform people of the death and the time of the funeral. A sin-eater might be taken on and paid so much for each sin absorbed from the corpse, duly washed down with a glass of whisky. Many families were dismayed at how great a sinner their relative appeared to have been.

Catholic priests at a walking funeral would stop at each crossroads and ask, "who will give me money for the sake of this man's soul?" and it was customary for the minister to receive as a croce present some item from the deceased's plenishing. Even today it is customary for the undertaker to give £1.00 to the hospital porter if the corpse has to be removed from the hospital mortuary to the chapel of rest and this is detailed on the final account.

At the draidgie, the after-funeral entertainment, a shilling was given by neighbours,

> *Oatcakes, shortbread, spirits and gin were served and every married woman was expected to attend and contribute a 1/- to help the widow or widower.*
>
> Newhaven Funerals in Olden Times

Servants were given money to dye material black and to buy gloves to wear at the funeral.

Debtors

Creditors by law could arrest a corpse in the seventeenth century and hold up the interment until the debts were paid.

To avoid this happening a widow could follow her husband's coffin to the door and call on him in the presence of mourners to return to pay off his debts. This relieved her of responsibility for them.

Taxes

A heriot or death tax was imposed by the Church before the Reformation, this usually consisted of cattle or horses. The inability to pay led to excommunication.

> *And when the Vikar hard tel my wyfe was dead*
> *The thrid cow he clekit by the head.*
> *The u'mest clayis that was o' the rapploch gray,*
> *The Vikar gart his clark bear them away.*
>
> *Works*, Sir David Lyndsay, 15--

If the widow had no animal to give then the "uppermost cloth" or blanket was taken from her bed. This was eventually forbidden by an Act of Parliament in 1617.

Dead-box

After friendly societies were set up in the nineteenth century they ensured that the cost of a funeral could come from the dead-box. In Dundee in the first decade of the twentieth century there were 10,000 women members of the Burial Society and it was equally popular in other industrial areas of Scotland.

When the Scots descended on England after the Union of the Crowns in 1603 they organised an earlier version, a Scots Box, into which they put contributions towards helping any one of them who fell on hard times. Three hundred Scots who died during the Great Plague were buried at its expense.

Alms-house bell

> *At every passing funeral, the little bell, in the turret of a*
> *little steeple, which projected as far as the kerbstone of the*
> *pavement was rung. In front of the turret was a stone*
> *tablet with the inscription "Give to the puir, and thou*

shalt have treasure in Heaven." In this tablet was a slit,
with, at one time a box behind it, but which latterly was
removed; boys in the latter days, being in the practice of
dropping bits of slate into the slit.

Glasgow and its Clubs, John Strang, 1864

Bell-pennies

To frighten away evil spirits the passing-bell was tolled at
whatever hour of the day or night the death occurred. Before
the days of the friendly societies folk saved bell-pennies to pay
for their funeral and also to give to the bell-ringer. He also
tolled the bell at the time of the funeral. Sometimes it was
hung from the branches of a tree at the entrance to the
graveyard. Mourners placed silver coins, called burial silver,
in a plate to defray the expenses.

Deid-dole

The deid-dole was given to beggars and students after a
funeral, usually in the form of food, although sometimes
money was given. Whenever a funeral was heralded by the
bellman the poor came from far and near to fight for a portion.

The professional beggars, licensed or not licensed, were
ever on the alert for alms – they swarmed at marriages,
and they swarmed at funerals. At these latter occasions
after the guests had partaken of the ale and shortbread,
and oatcakes before the lifting, the poor partook of the food
which was provided for them; and such items mentioned in
the old household account books as "12 dozen bread for the
poor" on the occasion of a burial show that their share in
the post mortem charity was very considerable.

The Social Life of Scotland in the 18th Century, H.G. Graham, 1899

This custom stems from the Catholic era when alms were
originally given to the poor to pray for the soul of the dead.
Sometimes if the beggars were displeased with the amount
provided they would hold the area up to ransom, demanding
money and valuables from the inhabitants.

Passed away

The moment of death was fraught with danger for the spirit of the dear departed. No matter that all forms of Christianity taught that the soul was safe in the everlasting arms, the people of Scotland were not to be fooled. The devil and his minions were waiting to seize the departing spirit as it set out on its last journey. Although many people prepared the way for the exit of the spirit, at the same time they hedged their bets by accepting the contrary view, which many believed, that the spirit did not leave the body but hovered over it until it was safely interred, and therefore it must be guarded at all times. This can be accounted for by the Celtic dual belief that there was an animal spirit within everyone and this guarded the body while the ghost spirit or soul took flight heavenwards immediately.

Pagan customs

Rushlights burned in the single room, and the door and the window stood open. It was a miserable hut of unmortared stones from the hill, the gaps stuffed with earth and turf, and the roof of heather thatch. One glance showed him that he was too late. A man sat on a stool by the dead peat-fire with his head in his hands. A woman was moving bedside the box bed unfolding a piece of coarse linen. The shepherd of the Greenshiel might be an old exercised Christian, but there were things in that place which had no warrant from the Bible. A platter full of coarse salt lay at the foot of the bed, and at the top crossed twigs of ash.

Witchwood, John Buchan, 1922

This passage includes many of the actions which had to be taken to avert the possibility of evil spirits interfering with the dead. Normally the nearest relative bent over the dying person to receive the last breath. When it was ascertained that death had occurred the clock was stopped or at least the chiming mechanism was removed. All mirrors and pictures were covered, preferably with black cloth or white linen, to prevent the spirit going in the wrong direction. Curtains and blinds were closed, fires put out and doors and windows opened so as not to impede the fleeing spirit.

Wasted, weary, wherefore stay,
restling thus with earth and clay?
From the body pass away;-
Hark! the mass is singing.

From these doff thy mortal weed,
Mary Mother be thy speed,
Saints to help thee at thy need;-
Hark! the knell is ringing.

Fear not snow-drift driving fast,
Sleet or hail or levin blast;
Soon the shroud shall lap thee fast,
And the sleep be on thee cast
That shall know no waking.

Haste thee, haste thee, to be gone,
Earth flits fast, and time draws on,—
Gasp thy gasp, and groan thy groan
Day is near the breaking.

Heaven cannot abide it,
Earth refuses to hide it,
Open lock — end strife,
Come death, and pass life.
    Guy Mannering, Sir Walter Scott, 1829

In Galloway bee skeps were adorned with black ribbons and in other Lowland areas the hive was covered with black crepe and the bees told of the death to prevent them swarming or ceasing to produce honey. It was believed that bees were the messengers of the gods.

Sometimes a professional mourning woman walked behind the coffin wailing.

*In Tiree the mourning woman was found until the middle
of the last century. The bean-tuiream followed the body,
every now and then striking the coffin with her hands like
a drum, and making all the din possible, and keeping time
with the movements of the men. All the virtues of the dead,
and a few more, were mentioned and extolled and the
genealogy for many generations praised and lauded.*

Carmina Gadelica, Alexander Carmichael, 1899

These women often doubled as the local midwife and the
community ensured that they were always supplied with
summer grass and winter fodder. The custom is a continuation
of the old Druid belief that it was important for the lineage of
the corpse to be known.

Sometimes the house door was painted black and silver
paper tears stuck on to it or white paint splashes to represent
tears. On other occasions the church door received this
treatment. This custom originated in France and was adopted
by those of high standing in Scotland to show the affliction of
the family for the loss of the departed.

*For colouring and tearing the church doors and lettering
them and colouring and tearing the wall opposite to your
burial-place and lettering the same. (account to the Laird
of Murdiston) 1742.*

The Social Life of Scotland in the 18th Century, H.G. Graham, 1899

Pets

Before death occurred all cats, dogs or budgies would have
been put out of the room. It was believed that witches and
wicked spirits adopted the forms of animals and might harm
the corpse. It was also important to prevent an animal jumping
over the corpse or the devil would have control of its spirit.

Laying out

If the eyes were open they had to be closed as the departing
spirit might seek a companion. No one would look a corpse in

the eye. Coins were placed on the eyelids to keep them closed. In some areas an iron nail was put into butter and cheese to prevent them going rancid and milk was poured on the ground.

When the corpse was laid out a plate of salt was placed on the breast to prevent the swelling of the body, or so it was believed. However in earlier times it also acted as a barrier against the devil for neighbours and family to come to touch the corpse, which was supposed to banish the ghost of the person from their mind. Children also took part in this custom. Touching a dead body was thought to be a cure for warts too.

> *James Hodge, who lives in the first close above the cross, on the west side of the High Street, continues to sell burying-crapes ready-made; and his wife's niece, who lives with him, dresses dead corpses at a cheap rate as was formerly done by her aunt, having been educated by her and perfected at Edinburgh, from whence she has lately arrived and has brought with her all the latest and newest and best fashions.*
>
> Advertisement, 1747

Deid-claes

Before there were undertakers to take control the family and neighbours carried out all the necessary tasks such as washing the body, anointing it with oil and laying it out. The deid-claes were often kept ready. In olden times the first duty of the young married wife when housekeeping began was to sew the dead clothes for herself and her husband. It was the custom to air them regularly, sometimes even washing them and hanging them out on the washing line.

> *The woman – she was a neighbouring shepherd's wife – stilled her keening at the sound of David's feet. "It's himsel'" she cried. "Richie, it's the minister. Wae's me sir, but ye're ower late to speed puir Mirren. An hour syne she gaed to her reward – just slipped awa' in a fit o' hostin'. I've strauchten'd the corp and am gettin' the deid claes*

ready – Mirren was aye prood o' hers and keepit them fine
and caller, wi' gall and rosm'ry Come forrit, sir, and tak
a look on her that's gane There was nae deid-thraws wi'
Mirrin, and she's peaceful as a bairn.

Witchwood, John Buchan, 1922

It was also customary to place woollen stockings, often white, and shoes on the feet of the corpse. This custom was part of the Catholic Church's belief in the Brigg o' Dread over which the soul had to travel and the thorny path along which it had to journey.

This ae nighte, this ae nighte,
Every night and alle;
Fire and sleete and candle lighte,
And Christ receive thy saule. . .

If ever thou gavest hosen and shoon
Every nighte and alle;
Sit thee down and put them on;
And Christ receive thy saule.

If hosen and shoon thou ne'er gavest nane,
Every nighte and alle;
The whinnies shall prick thee to thy bare bane:
And Christ receive thy saule. . .

From Brigg o' Dread when thou mayest passe,
Every nighte and alle;
To purgatory fire thou comest at laste;
And Christ receive thy saule.

If ever thou gavest meat or drink,
Every nighte and alle;
The fire shall never make thee shrink,
And Christ receive thy saule.

If meate or drinke thou never gavest nane,
Every nighte and alle;
The fire will burn thee to the breast bane;
And Christ receive thy saule.

The Lyke-wake Dirge, traditional ballad

Acts of Parliament

The government from time to time passed Acts of Parliament which ruled that winding sheets had to be made of certain materials to help manufacturers. In 1694 an Act decreed the use of linen which in turn was repealed in 1705 to be replaced by another Act requiring Scots woollen cloth to be used to support the woollen industry. A fine was imposed for breaking the rule. The wealthier citizens ignored the rules and paid up, preferring to be clad in satin or velvet or at least allowing the ladies a touch of lace.

The paupers though had no choice and were grateful to certain benefactors who provided them with a shroud, many of them travelling miles to die in an area where it was known that a decent burial would be arranged.

Stopping work

It was customary for all outside work to stop as a mark of respect whenever a death occurred in the community. The cessation lasted until the funeral rites were completed.

Funeral Undertakers

During the cholera outbreak of 1832 in Glasgow the authorities had difficulty in finding anyone to remove the dead. Two young carpenters who volunteered to bury the bodies never looked back, offering their services to anyone who required them and became undertakers. Their names were Mr. Wylie and Mr Lochhead whose firm has organised funerals in the city ever since.

Coffins

Before undertakers were employed the local joiner would arrive carrying his dead-deal, or streaking board to straighten out the corpse. Occasionally if the death thraws had been violent the bones would be twisted and would need to be broken before being straightened and measured for the coffin.

The joiner made and delivered the coffin which lay surrounded by candles until the service. There are fewer joiners now making coffins and in rural areas and small towns a corpse may still need to lie for up to thirty-six hours before a coffin is delivered from the nearest city.

Materials for coffins

Coffins, known as black breeks, have been made from many types of wood. Oak has always been a favourite and it was believed that if anyone was buried in an oak coffin, the hair would not decay but continue to grow.

At one time lead was used because of its preservative properties but was sore on the shoulders of the bearers. The parish chest had a hinged bottom and was used over and over in the eighteenth century at the burial of paupers.

> *The session of Rothesay desiderates yet the want of ane engyne to convey the coffin. . . to the grave with the corps. Therefore appointed John McNeil, thesaurer, to agree with the smith to make and join to the said chest a loose iron cleek fit for receiving a man's hand at everie end, and appoints the same chest when finished to be recommended to the kirk officer; and he is strictly appointed to take particular care that the said chest when used be in no way damaged.*
> The Social Life of Scotland in the 18th Century , H.G. Graham, 1899

Trestles

The coffin rested on wooden trestles which were supplied by the undertaker. If none was available then two wooden chairs could support it. The lid was left open until the last minute so that anyone visiting could be invited to view the corpse. Undertakers, especially in the cities, began to use cosmetics to enhance the appearance of the corpse to such an extent that they often looked healthier dead than alive.

Coffins became elaborate being lined with satin and the simple shroud of olden days gave way to the best clothes made of expensive materials. Many people chose highly ornate coffins with brass scrolls. Handles which used to be of wood were of brass and came in a wide variety of styles. Often the relatives, sometimes at the wish of the deceased, put on a show of wealth to impress those in attendance and emphasise their status.

Death at sea

If someone died at sea the sailmaker would fashion a canvas shroud and sew the body into it, placing the last stitch through the nose to ensure that there was no life left in it. If a body was washed up on a shore it was buried between the high and low tideline as it was considered dangerous to offend the spirits of the sea by depriving them of their rights. It was considered unlucky to save a man from drowning as it was taking from the sea what was its by right. This was a throwback to pagan times when it was believed that the sea demanded a human sacrifice.

Wakes and kistings

The Catholic lykewake, or sitting with the corpse until the time of its burial, was one of the popish customs which continued after the Reformation. To leave the corpse in the dark would lead it to the road to hell so candles had to be kept lit at all times of the day and night. If a candle blew out it bode ill for the one who lit it and deid-spales, the candle-grease on a guttering candle which assumed a shroud-like shape, was supposed to be a warning of the death of the person in whose direction it formed.

> *"God sain him!" said the women. The men took off their bonnets. "May the Possessor keep him in his keeping!" they said. . . Some went up to the White House and sat the night through with candles around*

*the body, silent and discreet for the sake of herself and
Father Ludovick, though in any other house in Uist they
would have passed the evening differently. At morning
too, others came with funeral gifts – cake, halibut and
fowls; and the day was silent with no noise of looms or
oars, as if it had been a day of Obligation.*

Children of Tempest, Neil Munro, 1895

Often it was the young folks who volunteered to sit up all
night, comforted by spiritual refreshments, usually whisky.
They passed the time telling ghost stories and the sensitive
mind began to creep with fear. On occasions, by accident, the
corpse would move as a result of the natural gases leaving
the body and an arm might flop down, or moans be heard.
Sometimes it was a practical joke with one of the company
creeping underneath and tipping the bier up.

During the seventeeth and eighteenth centuries when
Acts determining the type of material for the winding-sheet
were in force the Kirk decreed that an elder must be present
when the corpse was transferred into its coffin so that he
could check that the rules were obeyed. This led to him
being accompanied by the minister who put up a prayer for
the bereaved. In Presbyterian Scotland no prayers were
said for the dead as they were assured of a place in heaven,
being of the elect. This occasion was also observed by
relatives and neighbours and was called the kisting. It took
the place of the wake and developed into a gathering of the
women who sat around gossiping and drinking tea or
sometimes something stronger. By the nineteenth century
this had ceased but often two or three people would keep a
watch in a more seemly manner and without the drinking
and dancing.

Funeral dances

Death was not always a solemn occasion. At one time it was a
cause for rejoicing that the spirit was released and about to rise

to a better life on high, with relatives dancing around the corpse while weeping at their loss.

In some parts of the country, in the nineteenth century, the funeral dances were still kept up. These began on the evening of the death. All the neighbours attended the summons, and the dance, accompanied by a lament, was begun by the nearest relatives who were joined by all those present. This was repeated every evening until the interment to keep evil powers away.

Guisers

Another custom was that of guisers who visited the dead-house to beg for alms. This was usually a group of boys demanding food or money for the sake of the corpse's soul.

> Guising at funerals was forbidden by Chuch and State, who were united in their efforts to weed out the gross superstition by which the populace was still enslaved. In the Records of Inverness, as well as those of the Priory Council there are many references to the subject and to punishment of the offenders. The custom died out in most parts of the country by the 1840s.
>
> The Silver Bough, Vol 3, F. M. McNeill, 1961

Dig my grave and let me lie

In very early times islands, such as Inchcailleach on Loch Lomond, were a favourite place to have a burial ground as they gave protection from wild animals, especially wolves.

When most people lived in the country or in small towns the church had its own burying ground. The graves nearest the church door were filled first then east, south and west but the north corner of a kirkyard was the least desirable area and was often kept for the burying of unbaptised babies or the stillborn. In some areas it was the men from the next village who would come to dig the grave; in others members of the family carried out this task. By the late nineteenth century gravediggers were appointed who looked after the garden area and tended the graves as well as digging new lairs and opening up older ones as required.

Cemeteries

As the agricultural and industrial revolutions brought changes to the pattern of life many people moved to towns which put pressure on the limited facilities for burial and land was bought, usually on the outskirts of the town or city, by private companies to provide cemeteries which were generally non-denominational.

Families purchased lairs which when dug could house up to six coffins. Some bought double lairs. In prestigious cemeteries such as the Glasgow Necropolis, opened in 1832 and owned by the Merchants House, the great and the good chose to be buried in mausoleums, sarcophagi of Peterhead granite and in large vaults. Each monument was more ornamental than its neighbour. The entrances and waiting rooms of many cemeteries were elaborate and usually of classical design. By the end of the century, however, local authorities took over the running of cemeteries.

Crematoria

In 1932 the Merchants House of Glasgow submitted plans for a crematorium to the Secretary of State for Scotland but nothing came of this proposal. By the 1950s, however, cremation was gaining favour and several crematoria were functioning. This method of disposing of the dead by reducing the body to ashes has its own customs, but it separates the living from actual participation in the placing of the body in its final resting place.

Bodysnatchers

In the early nineteenth century there was much consternation because of the activities of the resurrectionists or bodysnatchers.

Students of anatomy required access to human bodies which were often in short supply and this led to a trade in stealing from newly opened graves at night after the interment. The infamous pair Burke and Hare took this one step further and murdered to supply sufficient fresh corpses. They were hanged in Edinburgh in 1829.

In many older kirkyards watch houses or gatehouses, where men would pass the night guarding the graves, can still be seen. There were fireplaces and chimneys so that they could keep warm. They were forbidden to drink alcohol and took turns, usually in pairs of arriving at sunset and remaining until dawn. Another deterrent was permanent cages over the grave or mort-safes which were made of cast iron and covered the grave during the vulnerable period. The practice ceased with the Anatomy Act of 1832.

Mourning dress

Black was not always worn at funerals. Many people could not afford to buy clothes specially for such an occasion and ordinary clothes were worn. At one time women even wore bright colours at funerals. After the undertakers took over the proceedings, especially in cities, it became de rigueur for those attending to wear black weeds, the women often heavily veiled in black lace.

Queen Victoria wore black, until her own death, in mourning for Prince Albert, her consort. The women of the upper classes who followed her fashion always dressed in black for a regulation period of a year after the death of a close relative. This was followed by the wearing of grey, then a touch of purple or lilac was permitted and finally a return to colours could occur. Special jewellery was worn, such as jet beads and mourning brooches which had a space at the back to insert a lock of the dead person's hair. Cameos and lockets also had a cavity for this purpose.

Men wore black arm bands called weepers, and a band of crepe tied around their hats. A black tie and black socks are usually kept as part of most men's wardrobes ready for wearing at funerals. On the death of a public figure people, even children, may wear black arm bands.

The lifting

This was the preliminary to the funeral. Invitations were sent out by word of mouth, the bell-man or black-edged and printed summonsing friends to the funeral. It was a mark of respect that everyone should have a decent burial and all local men had to attend. Food and drink was provided and, in the case of a poor man, the kirk session often helped to defray the expenses.

Scotland was until the agricultural and industrial revolutions of the mid eighteenth century an extremely egalitarian country, albeit a poor one. The Presbyterian Church preached that all men were equal in the sight of God and the laird attended the funerals of his farmers as readily as they attended his.

Although the invitation was for ten o'clock in the forenoon the corpse was never interred till the evening. . . The routine was as follows, a prayer was pronounced before and after the service. The service consisted of, first, a drink of ale, then a dram, then a piece of shortbread, then another dram. . . then a piece of currant bread and a third dram either of wine or spirits. This was followed by loaves and cheese, pipes and tobacco.

The Parish of Campsie, John Cameron, 1892

The lifting was often delayed until folk who had to come a distance had gathered. Many people chose to be buried where they were born which might be at some distance from where they now lived. Wherever the burial was to be it was usually a walking funeral where all the mourners walked to the graveside.

Deid-spokes

The men organised themselves into teams to carry the coffin, starting with the closest relatives and then the next group, usually of the younger relations. The coffin was covered with a mort-cloth of wool or linen usually hired from the kirk session at a fixed cost, though the wealthy often chose black velvet.

Poles or hand-spokes were slipped beneath the coffin on its trestles in the dead room and it was manoeuvred to the front door where two chairs had been placed ready to receive it. The first team would shoulder the coffin and set off, led by a piper with a black pennant tied to his pipes. Occasionally the women of the family would take the first lift, carrying the coffin for twenty to thirty yards. Usually there were eight bearers in two files and at a signal, without interrupting the march, the leading pair would slip their shoulders beneath the poles and the second pair would move up. Each pair in turn would be replaced by another until the team was completely changed. If anyone slipped and dropped the handspoke it was supposed to indicate that his own death might not be far off. However, on some occasions the mourners, having indulged too much, had difficulty steadying the coffin and tales of corpses dropped or forgotten are legion.

> *Yesterday we were invited to the funeral of an old lady, the grandmother of a gentleman in this neighbourhood, and found ourselves in the midst of fifty people who were regaled with a sumptuous feast, accompanied with the music of a dozen pipers. In short, this meeting had the air of a grand festival; and the guests did such honour to the entertainment, that many of them could not stand when they were reminded of the business on which we had met. The company forthwith taking horse, rode in a very irregular cavalcade to the place of interment, a church, at a distance of two long miles from the castle. On our arrival, however, we found we had committed a small oversight in leaving the corpse behind; so that we were obliged to wheel about and met the old gentlewoman half-way, carried upon poles by the nearest relations of her family.*
>
> Humphrey Clinker, Tobias Smollett, 1771

Cairns

It was often said by observers that a Scots funeral was merrier than an English wedding. If the journey was long, cairns were built along the way to rest the coffin on while a small refreshment was partaken. If the road was one regularly used by funerals then a stone was added to each cairn on passing. If the coffin had to be transported by a boat the special stones on which it rested on arrival on dry land were called leek-stanes.

Right of way

In some areas it was considered that if a coffin was regularly carried over a certain path it became a right of way.

The burial

Timing

The time of a burial was important and many interments were delayed in seaside communities until the tide was ebbing. Friday was not considered a good day for a burial.

Burial customs

In the early eighteenth century a burial was a civil and not a religious occasion, often it was not the minister who delivered the eulogy but a friend. The saying "never speak ill of the dead" was taken literally and folk often wondered if they were attending the right funeral. The firing of guns was a custom related to that of ringing bells, making of noise to chase away evil spirits.

As soon as the body was coffined, or in some places after the funeral, all bedding and the clothes worn by the deceased at the time of death were burned and in the case of cholera the whole house might be razed by fire. When the deceased died from cancer it was the custom to place butter on the corpse to draw out the tumour and the corpse go to its grave restored.

Sometimes amputated limbs were buried with the dead in case they were needed in heaven.

Sometimes food or items of clothing which might be needed in the other world were thrown into the grave to prevent the spirit of the corpse returning for those necessities. It is thought that throwing earth on top of the buried coffin might be a remnant of this custom rather than an embodiment of the words "earth to earth, ashes to ashes, dust to dust".

Women

At the burial ground or cemetery gates, the women turned homewards. It was uncommon for women to attend a graveside up until about the 1950s. Mainly they remained at home preparing for the return of the mourners and keeping the widow or widower company, as it was not the custom for a husband to attend his wife's burial until the nineteenth century. There were exceptions. At the funeral of the Scottish president of the British Women's Temperance Association in Alloa in 1915, women not only attended the burial but were pall-bearers.

Transport

As time went on the coffin was less often carried. Sometimes a wooden barrow was wheeled to the graveyard then later a horse and cart carried it. Gradually, as undertakers became more common, a horse-drawn vehicle called a hearse was specially built for the purpose of conveying the coffin in style. It had glass windows all round so that the coffin could be viewed, usually draped in black. In Victorian times it had the splendour of attendants wearing morning dress and top hats which were draped in black crepe and horses bedecked with black feather plumes.

In the twentieth century motorised hearses were introduced followed by large cars called limousines to carry the mourners.

Refreshments

The final part of the funeral came after the burial. Refreshments were served at what was called the draidgie, dregy or dirgie, another excuse for drinking and eating to excess. This was often held in the barn of the deceased's home or in the best room of the house, and was the time to wish the departed spirit a safe landing on the other side. The women who had stayed at home prepared the food. Sometimes there would be entertainment and even dancing. The custom survives in the form of a meal, traditionally of steak pie, served either at home or in a hotel or restaurant or a tea with sausage rolls, sandwiches and cakes to which those attending the funeral are invited from the pulpit by the minister. It is usually only close friends and relatives who remain for this part of the proceedings.

Announcements

In towns and cities by the twentieth century funerals had lost their significance to the whole community and were attended by relatives and friends, but an open invitation was, and still is, issued, nowadays usually in the form of an announcement in the local or national newspaper.

At one time these hatches, matches and dispatches, as the intimations were popularly called, appeared on the front page, but latterly they were moved inside. They inform when and where death took place and the day, time and place of the funeral. Acknowledgements are often placed in the paper after the funeral, thanking all those who have helped the bereaved in some way.

In Scotland the intimation of the death of a woman often includes her maiden name without the use of nee. Another custom is that of placing "In Memoriam". These remembrances, usually on the anniversary of a death, are often accompanied by sugary sweet and sentimental verses.

Deep in my heart,
Your memory is kept.
I smile at the world,
But will never forget.

Sympathy cards

Since the late nineteenth century friends and acquaintances sent sympathy cards to the family of the bereaved. Roman Catholics sent mass cards and lit candles in memory of the deceased. In 1816 it was customary to say "the black ox has trampled on ye" when first meeting the bereaved as a token of sympathy.

Floral tributes

Flowers were not always part of the ceremony and are rarely mentioned until the late nineteenth century. In the Highlands wreaths of heather were hand-made but large and ostentatious wreaths and floral arrangements only came into favour with the advent of hearses and undertakers. Even today the most amazing variety of flowers can be heaped on top of and around the coffin. The latest trend is to have a tribute with connections to the dear departed's interests. A guitar decorated with flowers or a football in the team colours or large letters, about a foot high, spelling out "Dad" or "Mum" or "Love" in flowers. These are more common at a burial and the request, "no flowers please", often appears on the intimation for a cremation when only a family wreath is generally present. In most cemeteries graves have flowers regularly placed on them by relatives of the dead throughout the year.

Public funerals

On the death of a public figure flags were flown at half mast on public buildings, a custom many bowling and golf clubs follow on the death of a member.

Public funerals throughout the years have been lavish occasions with pomp and pageantry.

A striking sight it must have been, that long heraldic procession which went before the body of the deceased

noble, along the banks of the Teviot, on that bright June
day. First there were forty-six saulies in black gowns and
hoods, with black staves in their hands, headed by one
called a conductor, who was attended by an old man in a
mourning gown; a trumpeter in the Buccleuch livery
following, and sounding his trumpet. Next came Robert
Scott of Howshaw, fully armed, riding on a fair horse,
and carrying on the point of a lance a little banner of the
defunct's colours, azure and or. Then a horse in black, led
by a lackey in mourning, a horse with a crimson velvet
foot-mantle, and three trumpets in mourning on foot,
sounding sadly. Then the great gumpheon, of black taffeta
carried on a lance by Walter Scott of Lauchope, his sword
borne by Andrew Scott of Broadmeadows, his gauntlets
by Francis Scott of Castleside, and his coat of honour by
Mr. Lawrence Scott.

The next great section of the procession was a purely
heraldic display. Eight gentlemen of the Clan Scott bore
each the coat of arms of one of the various paternal and
maternal ancestors of the defunct. Other gentlemen of
the name – Scott of Harden, Scott of Scotstarvet etc.
– carried the great pencil, the deceased's standard, his
coronet, and his arms in metal and colour, near whom
were three more trumpets and three pursuivants, all in
mourning. "Last of all cam the corps, carried under a
fair pall of black velvet, decked with arms, larmes (tears),
and cipress of sattin, knopt with gold, and on the coffin
the defunct's helmet and coronet, overlaid with cipress,
to shew that he was a soldier. And so in this order, with
the conduct of many honourable friends, marched they
from Branxholm to Hawick Church, where after the
funeral sermon endod, the corps were interred amongst
his ancestors."

Report of the funeral on the 11th June 1635 of the Earl of Buccleuch
who had died before Christmas the previous year in London. from
*Domestic Annals of Scotland, Vol 2 , From the Reformation to the
Revolution*, Robert Chambers, n.d.

The funeral of a Highland laird was also a cause for a large, spectacular turnout. All friends and kinsmen within a hundred miles attended, and all the retainers and vassals were present. The entertaining of guests continued for several days. A toastmaster was chosen from the company at the feast; the healths were drunk, although the thanks returned were not always coherent; liquor was emptied in hogsheads. At last, the cortège, miles long, would set out for the kirkyard, perhaps many miles away, with torches flaring, coronachs chanting, or pibrochs wailing.

Happy Death

In the earlier centuries the the Western Islands and in many parts of the Highlands the Catholic belief of the bas sona or happy death meant that the corpse had been confessed, anointed and the death hymn had been sung. The Presbyterians could not curb the celebratory approach to death, it took the stiff Victorians to set a seal of sorrow on this natural occasion.

LUCKY AND UNLUCKY

*L*ucky and unlucky usually mean having good or bad fortune. Although they are abstract terms, and there is no proof, throughout the centuries certain objects and actions were believed to have an influence on luck. If good luck followed its use then, in a self-fulfilling way, this was attributed to the magical properties of the object and as long as it was touched, carried or consulted good luck would occur. In the same way if bad luck happened then a certain object or action would be to blame.

Black and white magic became tied up in the old customs. Black magic included enchantment, the casting of the evil eye, and the influence of spirits who wished harm to humans and who blighted their crops and belongings; antidotes to this had to be found. White magic included fertility, love charms, good luck charms and carrying objects which guaranteed protection from evil. There were many customs to combat either but mainly the constant battle was against evil which seemed to lurk around every corner and to affect every step in life.

The evil eye

It was dreaded and was used by witches and those in league with the devil to blight crops, arrest childbirth and cause animals to go lame and their milk to dry up. The evil eye means to have the power of casting an envious glance on people and animals, causing them to sicken and die in a few hours. Some people who were not witches believed that they had the evil eye without knowledge of how this came about and were very aware of the havoc which they could cause unintentionally and often apologised for their affliction.

Ashes of rowan wood were scattered onto the windowsill to avert the evil eye. If an action was repeated on three consecutive Thursdays any spell could be broken.

Deaseil

One of the most common customs which appears throughout all facets of social behaviour is the action of going deaseil, by the right, the movement from east to west following the path of the sun. The sun was worshipped by the Druids and brought light, life and growth to the world. The opposite direction was widdershins, which is leftwise or against the sun and was the way of those who dealt in black magic. From passing the claret, stirring the porridge to approaching the church for any purpose the action must take place sunwise to ensure success. There is an old Gaelic saying: "Close the north window and quickly close the south, and close the window towards the west, evil never came from the east".

Cardinal points

However, there is a theory that turning by the right is not based on the journey of the sun but on the cardinal points, which played an important part in Highland custom, every move being influenced by them. The lucky turning is from the north (or left) by the east to the south (or right). The unlucky movement is tuaithea – leftwise, that is by north, west and south to the east – the widdershins turning. It is of interest to note that the rightwise turning is also that of the constellation of the Great Bear known in Gaelic as Grigirean – the clock. The pointer of this group faces north in winter, east in spring, south in summer and west in autumn.

Taking heed of the direction was important. For example facing south at sunrise when pulling herbs would make their power more potent. Flitting northwards it was considered lucky to set out on a Saturday but flitting southwards was best on a Monday. The north wind, called the black wind, was considered unlucky and a bringer of evil. All the cardinal points were associated with colours: north – black; south – white; west – brown and the east – purple, the sacred airt.

Talismen

Various types of objects and actions were thought to bring good luck. These were called talismen and stemmed originally from figures cut or engraved on metal or stone under the influence of the planets whose sympathetic power was believed to be transferred to the holder. This idea spread to include such items as stones, wands, relics, flags, crystals, horns and cups believed to possess magical powers which could be transferred to a person upon contact or could be used to bring success to a clan. Another category of talismen were standing or rocking stones and natural objects such as the sun, moon, stars, fire and water.

Unlucky objects and actions also existed and there were counter-charms to defeat these, often with spoken charms or runes, many of which are now lost. These were originally chanted by the Druids but many were Christianised and the names of saints, the Virgin Mary or the Trinity were substituted for those of the old gods and goddesses

Quarter Days

Luck could run out or be taken away and care had to be taken to preserve it. "The first monday of the Quarter take care that luck leave not thy dwelling". Quarter Days as the first day of each three monthly period was called, consisted of Candlemas (February), Whitsun (May), Lammas (August) and Martinmas (November) and it was only with great suspicion and care that anything was lent upon these days as the power of the supernatural was strongest at these times and the luck of the house might go with the item. These were also term days when rents were paid. They were supposed to be lucky days for many purposes such as starting a new fee. They coincide with the pagan festivals of Imloc, Beltane, Lammas and Samhain.

First footing took place on every quarter day. Neighbours carried a piece of coal or peat into the house for luck as well as wine or spirits which were shared out and everybody had to take a drink. This idea continues in that anyone visiting a new house for the first time takes along a small gift to handsel it and bring happiness and prosperity to the occupants. On every occasion on visiting friends a gift of home-made jam, home-baking, biscuits, sweets or flowers, often picked from your garden should be taken along. Often men take a bottle of spirits or wine for the host. In turn hospitality, in the shape of food and drink, is always offered to guests. It is an offence to refuse and is a throw back to the custom of giving bread and wine which was supposed to show that the visitor meant no harm and averted the influence of evil and brought prosperity to the house.

Stones

Many different types of stone were used in a variety of customs. It was believed that either a stone had a spirit of its own or that a spirit lived inside it. Large stones and small were imbued with the power to influence the course of events or bring about a cure for an illness and to seal bargains.

At some circles of standing stones, such as the Refuge Stone at Torphichen, criminals or debtors sought sanctuary and on reaching them were safe from harm. Stones such as crosses were deemed safe havens by royal command.

Macbeth being dethroned. Macduff demanded and obtained , first, that he and his successors, lords of

*Fife, should place the crown on the king's head at his
coronation; secondly; that they should lead the vanguard
of the army whenever the royal banner was displayed; and
lastly, this privilege of Clan Macduff whereby any person
being related to Macduff in the ninth degree, and having
committed homicide without premeditation, should upon
flying to Macduff's Cross and paying a certain fine, obtain
remission of their guilt.*

Minstrelsy of the Scottish Border, Sir Walter Scott, 1869

This cross stood near Lindores in Fife but was demolished
under instructions from John Knox, the reformer, and only
the pedestal remained. The cross was dedicated to St
Macgider and the surrounding tumuli are believed to contain
the bodies of those who could not prove their intentions to the
satisfaction of the Thane of Fife.

The town of Inverness has a stone, the Clach-na-Cudainn,
as its talisman.

Embedded at the foot of the Cross [The Town Cross in
the Exchange] *is the Clach-na-Cudainn (Stone of the
Tubs) regarded in tradition palladium. . . safeguard of the
town. Its traditions have grown with its centuries of
association with the town's historic past. One tradition
is that the stone was once the seat of a famous seer, who
prophesised that so long as the townsfolk of Inverness
preserved it the Burgh would flourish and be prosperous.*

The Book of the Highlands, 1933

Oaths

These were often sworn while a hand was laid on a specific
stone. An egg-shaped stone owned by Clan Chattan on the
Isle of Arran was used for the swearing of oaths and the
Stone of Destiny, on which kings are crowned, was chosen
for this purpose because it originally was called Lia Fail, or
the speaking stone, and it was supposed to name who should

be chosen as king. Originally it was used for the crowning of the king of Scotland, but it was taken from Scone by Edward 1, the Hammer of the Scots, in 1296. It is not certain whether the stone underneath the Coronation Chair in Westminster Abbey is the original, which according to legend was brought from Egypt and placed in the Abbey of Scone, or a replica, as it was stolen by Scottish partisans in 1951 and later recovered.

As the monarch is crowned an oath is taken. Oaths were taken on stones throughout Scotland and these oaths were as binding as any made before a magistrate. If anyone should default then ill-luck would follow. The Stone of Angus in Balquhidder, Perthshire, the Blackstone in the grounds of the cathedral at Iona, Odin's Stone in Orkney which had a natural fissure through which hands were joined to clinch a deal have been recorded as being some of many used for these purposes. Unfortunately this stone at Stenness was broken up in 1814 by a local farmer to use in a dyke. Even such serious matters as betrothal and marriage performed at a stone were binding, as long as there were two witnesses.

When a new chief of a clan was being installed he stood on a cairn or rock. Sometimes this would have footsteps cut out on it, in which he stood to swear that he would follow in the footsteps of his ancestors. He was then given the white wand, usually of yew, symbolic of power and a replica of that used by the Druids, the sword and clothed in the white robe of faithfulness, all of which previously belonged to his predecessor.

Boundary stones

Another stone in Iona was said to guarantee the owner the skill to steer a ship safely when an arm was waved over it three times, while boundary stones such as the Lochmaben Stone in Dumfriesshire were often assembling places for troops, and where deals, truces and judgements took place. The gallows tree was often nearby.

Boundary stones were often originally the burial cairn of some warrior and like many stones gained a reputation for having special powers. It was customary to put a madman behind a rider on a grey horse and gallop like the wind towards a boundary stone that had to be ridden round in a circle deaseil in order to effect a cure.

Foundation stones

In the time of the Picts the foundation stone of a building was bathed in human blood in propitiation to the spirit of the soil. If this custom was not observed it was believed that the work that was done by day would be undone by night. This custom continued in the form of burying a dead animal beneath a foundation stone and many bones have been discovered during the demolition of old buildings.

Gargoyles

Gargoyles with horrendously ugly faces embellished eaves and rooflines, especially of churches, to frighten away the devil. Stone figures decorated gateposts for the same purpose.

Pilgrimages

People regularly made pilgrimages to stones where they left votive offerings in the same way as was the custom at wells. One of these was the obelisk on the island of Berneray where coloured pebbles, coins, bone pins and bronze needles have been found and at Balintore, Ross and Cromarty, nobody would pass by the Ghosts Hillock unless they threw a stone into the hollow for luck.

Healing stones

To discover if a patient would recover from an illness "unspoken" water, taken in silence from under a bridge over which the living and the dead must pass, and which must not be spilled, was poured over a corner stone of a building, naming the patient. If the stone split it meant that the illness was fatal.

Smaller stones were also treated as talismen and believed to have magical properties and were in demand for healing disease in humans and cattle. Some clans had their own particular stone, many of which, along with crystals, were brought to Scotland from the East by returning crusaders during the Middle Ages. These are jealously guarded and some are mounted as brooches, necklaces and bracelets but are often also used by dipping them into water to which the power of the stone is transferred and the water is then taken to the source of need.

Another stone was plunged into almond oil and licked every morning for three weeks which resulted in a loss of weight and a stone bound on the pulse of the left wrist while chanting the Lord's Prayer was a cure for hysterics.

Children were thought to be cured of mumps and rickets by passing them beneath Logan or rocking stones. One in the Stewartry of Kirkcudbright weighed ten tons but was so well balanced that it could be rocked by a child. St Fillan's Chair, which was a natural rock hollow, appeared in two different locations, the first at Loch Earn in Perthshire and the second at Kilallan near Houston in Renfrewshire.

> *The rock on the summit of the hill, formed of itself a chair for the saint, which still remains. Those who complain of rheumatism in the back, must ascend the hill, sit in this chair, then lie down on their back, and be pulled by the legs to the bottom of the hill. This operation is still performed and reckoned very efficacious.*
>
> Old Statistical Account of Scotland, Perthshire, 1792

The very same description of the custom exists in both places and the action, while drastic, was reported as still practised in the early twentieth century.

Passing through a cleft rock is supposed to cleanse and heal wounds. Earthfast or insulated stones enclosed in a bed of earth were supposed to cure strains and bruises. These stones were of very hard material and were used to make axes which struck a fatal blow to an enemy.

St Columba's stone

This blue stone found in Skye was credited in legend with curing Briochan the Druid by being immersed in water and thereafter it was always damp. The water in which it was steeped was then drunk or bathed in as a cure for a stitch in the side. One of these stones was incorporated into the altar of the chapel on the Isle of Troda. When fishermen were becalmed they washed this stone to procure a favouable wind.

The Lee Penny

In 1330 Sir Simon Lockhart of Lee set out from Montrose to accompany James. Lord Douglas who was charged with returning the heart of King Robert the Bruce to the Holy Land. They travelled through Spain where Douglas was killed in a fight with the Moors. Lockhart proceeded to Palestine where he fought the Saracens and captured an emir, a Saracen chief, whose mother begged him to release her son. She dropped a coin from her purse and Lockhart realised that it was of great importance to her and demanded it as part of the deal for the release of her son.

Thus he gained possession of a cornelian, a dark red stone set in a silver coin which he had seen to have miraculous powers. He brought it home where its fame grew and it was a much-sought-after charm handed down through generations and called the Lee Penny. In the seventeenth century Gavin Hamilton of Raploch pursued a complaint against Sir James Lockhart of Lee at the General Assembly about the superstitious uses of the stone. Its verdict was as follows:

> The Assemblie having inquired of the manner of using thereof and particularly understood, be examination of the said Laird of Lee and otherwise, that the custom is only to cast the stone in some water, and give the diseasit cattle therof to drink, and that the same is done without using any words, such as the Charmers and Sorcerers use in their

*unlawful practices and considering that in nature thair are
many things seen to work strange effects, wherof no human
wit can give a reason, it having pleased God to give to
stones and herbs a special vertue for healing of many
infimities in man and beast, advises the Brethern to
surcease thair process as therin they percieve no ground of
Offence, and admonishes the Laird of Lee, in the using of
the said stone, to take heid that it be usut herafter with
the least scandle.*

Extract out of the Books of the Assemblie holden at Glasgow,
and subscribed at thair command by M. Robert Young,
Clerk to the Assemblie, 21st October 1630

It was one of the few stones accepted as valid by the Church
of Scotland when the General Assembly tried to have those
who used these magical stones for healing purposes charged
with a criminal offence. Bottles of the water in which it had
steeped were often hung over the byre door for protection
against the evil eye.

Glenbuckie Stone

The Stewarts of Advorlich in Perthshire had a stone called the
Glenbuckie Stone which was a wishing stone. The lady of the
house would dip the stone in water then walk three times round
the vessel which the guest took, drank and made a silent wish.
This family also owned a red stone known as Clach Dhearg
which was known to heal the diseases of cattle if steeped in a
pail of water and then taken out and carried three times round
the pail sunwise. People came for miles around to obtain some
of the water in which it was steeped to take back to their crofts.

Lucky stones

Self-bored stones were stones through which water had made
holes and were often referred to as elf cups. These were held
together with string or horse hair, often in threes and were
hung above the stable door as a protection against fairies,
usually on May the second. On Iona little green pebbles were

treasured as a protection against drowning. Serpent's stones
were formed when two snakes entangled and hissed at each
other, their spittle hardening and forming a ring of glass
which was highly prized as ensuring wealth for the finder.
Adder stones were often incorporated into the hilt of a sword
to protect the warrior.

It might have been thought that the doughty Covenanters
would have scorned all idea of extra-terrestrial influence but
Gordon of Rothiemay records that in 1639 a strange event
took place at Dunse Law while the Army of the Covenant
were camped there.

> *The falling of a part of the bank upon the steep side of the
> hill near by to the Scottish camp, which of its own accord
> had shuffled downwards, and by its fall discovered
> innumerable stones, round, for the most part, in shape,
> and perfectly spherical, some of them oval-shapen. They
> were of a dark grey colour, some of them yellowish, and
> for quantity they looked like ball of all sizes, from a pistol
> filed piece such as sakers or robenets, or battering- pieces
> upwards Smooth they were, and polished without but
> lighter than lead by many degrees, so that they were only
> for show, but not for use. Many of them were carried
> about in men's pockets, to be seen for the rarity. Nor
> wanted there a few who interpreted this stone magazine
> at Dunse Hill as a miracle, as if God had sent this by
> ane hid providence for the use of the Covenanters; for at
> this time all things were interpreted for the advantage
> of the Covenant.*
>
> Domestic Annals of Scotland, Vol 2, From the *Reformation*
> *to the Revolution,* Robert Chambers, n.d.

In Lanarkshire at Tinto near the source of the River Clyde
there was supposed to be a magic cup which was a hollow
stone filled with water.

> *On Tintock tap there is a mist,*
> *And in that mist thee is a kist,*

And in that kist there is a caup,
And in that caup there is a drap.
Tak up that caup, drink aff the drap
And set the caup on Tintock tap.

Legend had it that it was the thumbmark of William Wallace who was supposed to have thrown the stone.

Unlucky stones

Some stones were unlucky and were used to prevent good luck in conjunction with a curse.

It was at one time a common custom for a farmer who was
evicted, or who was leaving his farm under a sense of
grievance to fill up the fireplace in every room with broken
bottles and old stones and to lay on his successor a curse
which should never be lifted until these fires burned. When
the stone fires had been laid and the curse said, the doors
were locked and the tenant made his way out by the
window, the curse lighting upon the first person who
entered by thereafter. . . It was said that the incoming
tenant did not thrive.

    Highways and Byways in Galloway and Carrick, C.H. Dick, 1927

Bones

Bones were also considered to be talismen and to bestow good luck. Some of these were relics from the saints, especially arm bones which worked by transferring power to the arm of a warrior. They were often encased in a casket lined with velvet and bound with leather and silver called a reliquary. The arm bone of St Fillan was supposed to have been carried along the ranks of the kneeling Scottish army by the Abbot of Inchaffray before the Battle of Bannockburn in 1314 and the arm bone of St Giles is preserved in his cathedral in Edinburgh, resting in an ornate reliquary provided by the city fathers. Described as "a harden bag, near full of beads", a bag filled with pieces of bones, tied with a red thread and wrapped in silk and having the name of the saint which they belonged to attached to them, was found at Traquair House in the borders.

Skulls and skeletons

Our ancestors were not squeamish. When a criminal was hanged on the gallows tree, usually near a crossroads or boundary, the body was allowed to hang until it was a skeleton and bones taken from this were considered to have healing powers, as did the bones of an unbaptised child. Witches were supposed to treasure the skin of such an infant and use it in their foul deeds and they also used fat taken from the same source.

The skull of a suicide was eagerly sought after and treasured. It was supposed to be dug up after sunset and before sunrise to be used as a vessel for water from a holy well. If it was given to an epileptic to drink and the operation was conducted in silence a cure would result. The Well of the Head in Wester Ross has a legend about a woman buried on the moor whose skull involuntarily appeared above ground. It was taken and preserved in a silver casket with a Dewar or guardian, a wise man, who used it to carry out cures for epileptics. This ritual was still carried out in the twentieth century.

The patient and his or her companions had to go to the house of the guardian. The patient climbed the hill alone with the guardian, where the ceremony had to be carried out after the sun had left the hill, and before it reached it again. Complete silence had to be observed both on the long climb to the well, and on the return. Once the well was reached the recipient was instructed in the correct ritual, violation of which would ruin all chances of a cure. The skull was taken from its box and the well approached. The patient had to walk three times deaseil. The guardian then dipped the skull in the water and gave it to the suffering person in the name of the Trinity; this he did three times. He then put "prohibitions" on the patient, things he must never do, which were not divulged. The patient had to believe in the possibility of a cure. This particular custom is recorded in less formal circumstances at several wells.

Love potions

A crooked bone taken from a frog, which had to be killed on St John's Eve, June the twenty fourth, cleaned and dried over a fire of rowan and then powdered, was considered to be a love potion. It was sprinkled on food and was believed to gain the recipient's affection. It was also used to bring about a reconciliation after a quarrel.

Lucky bones

Some bones in the body were considered lucky, such as the front of the big toe of the right foot, the nail joints and the left foot of old men and should be touched for luck. The breastbones of fowls are split by two people pulling them when dried. The person with the largest portion makes a wish in silence and must not disclose the wish. The bone is more commonly known as the wishbone.

Unlucky bones

A witch wishing to bring harm took her cursing bone, often a small hollow bone of a deer, to the hen-house of her victim after sunset and before dawn. She wrung the neck of a hen and poured its blood through the bone as she cursed the dwelling.

Tooth fairy

Placing a tooth beneath a pillow for the tooth fairy to take away still occurs at a much inflated rate of exchange. Instead of a silver threepenny bit the fairy now leaves a pound coin. In some parts of Scotland it was supposed to be a mouse which took away the tooth and left gold or silver.

Cups

A cup believed to be blessed with supernatural powers was the Macmillan cup at Balmaghie in Galloway, the communion cup of the Reverend John Macmillan, first minister of the Reformed Presbyterian Church. The cup was treasured by a disciple of this covenanting sect in the parish of Kirkcowan, Galloway and used as a test of the conviction of the suspected persons. If, on taking the precious relic into his hand, the person trembled or gave other symptoms of agitation he was denounced as an unbeliever.

St Margaret introduced the custom of the loving cup to Scotland. This was passed round the table sunwise and all present had to drink from it to show friendship. If anyone refused they were considered an enemy or traitor.

A special toast used by Highland regiments and drunk from regimental crystal was the Highland Honours when, in full dress uniform, the officers stood with one foot on the floor and the other on the table to drink the health of the regiment. A secret toast in Jacobite times involved the cup being passed over the water jug to signify allegiance to Bonnie Prince Charlie, the King over the Water.

Severed head

The cult of the severed head was widespread in prehistoric times and our ancestors indulged in the dreadful practice of preserving the head as a relic. These heads were often placed in neuks on a staircase. The head of St Marnock was adopted by the Innes clan who lived at Aberchirder in Banffshire and it was paraded through the village when good weather was required. Lights were placed around it every Sunday and the relic was regularly washed and the water caught in a dish and bottled for healing purposes. The head of St Fergus was treasured at Scone where King James IV had a silver casket made for it.

Known as the Children of the Mist, the Clan MacGregor plundered and murdered with total disregard. In the sixteenth century some of the clan had killed John Drummond, a King's Forester, which led to the outlawing of the clan by the Scottish Government.

*The MacGregors who had committed the murder were
from Balquhidder, of the outlawed race known as the
Children of the Mist. They carried the gory head along
the wooded shore of Loch Earn and when they had
reached Balquhidder, sought out their chief, Alasdair
of Glenstrae, then a young man of twenty-one, and
flung themselves on his protection. Glenstrae took their
side. He summoned the clan, and in the old church of
Balquhidder a grim scene was enacted on a dark
autumn day. . . The head of the King's Forester was
placed upon the high altar, and the chief, walking
forward, laid his hands upon it and swore that he
would defend with his life those who had done the deed.
His clansmen followed his example, and the hearts of
the murderers were lightened as they saw that they
would not go friendless.*

Hyways and Byways in the Central Highlands, Seton Gordon, 1948

Croziers

Croziers were the staffs which bishops and also saints carried.
Several of these became treasured relics after their owner's
death. Many of them disappeared at the time of the
Reformation, such as the staff of St Donnan which had
worked miracles of healing in Auchterlees, Aberdeenshire. St
Fergus's staff was used to calm storms in Buchan and that of
St Fillan is preserved in the Scottish National Museum in
Edinburgh and was one of the relics which inspired the
Scottish army at Bannockburn. The crozier of St Moluag,
once kept at Lismore and later at Inveraray by the Duke
of Argyll, was carried for good fortune in battle in front of
the army of the men of Lorne; a hereditary custodian was
appointed and given a croft in which to live at Kilmun, near
Dunoon, as he guarded the staff of St Mund. Great store was
set on the efficacy of these holy relics to bring luck to those
who came under their jurisdiction.

Amulets

Amulets were used as protection. They were worn or carried upon the person or carefully placed in a house or byre to ward off evil. Bracelets were popular, some made of leather, others of copper, plaited hair or red coral. Necklaces were made which incorporated lucky stones, and pebbles were strung and worn by babies, children and adults.

It was believed that if these were worn at all times dangers such as death by drowning, lightning or attacks by robbers could be avoided. That luck would stay with the person under all circumstances and they would be successful in commercial dealings. Many objects were carried for luck: coins, charms, rabbit's foot, thread and iron, while rowan was sewn into the hems of clothing. Cattle and horses had items attached to their bodies as well as placed above their stall or stable or over the door.

Plants

Buttercups placed in a bag and hung around the neck were thought to cure insanity. An amulet of senna, mint and rue worn as a bracelet averted evil, as did primroses and convolvulus picked on May the first and twined into wreaths. In Moray woodbine cut on the waxing moon was made into hoops which were preserved until the following March. When children were sick they were passed through one three times to effect a cure.

Thread and hair

These were often used as amulets but could also be used by witches to bring ill-luck. Twined threads tied with nine knots each sealed with spittle and chanted over with a special rune was a cure for lameness in beasts but a witch could bring this about using the same items. Equally if a witch could obtain a hair from her victim she could cast spells over them so it was important to burn hair after it was cut; finger and toenail cuttings had also to be treated with care for the same reason. Threads tied with three knots, by a wise woman, were taken to sea by fishermen. If they wished a light breeze they untied one knot, a second gave them a strong breeze but the third must not be undone or a storm would arise. Witches conjured up a storm by chanting over a stone as they thrashed it with a knotted rag.

> *I knot this ragg upon this stane,*
> *To raise the wind in the Devillis name;*
> *It sall not lye till I please againe.*
>
> Traditional rhyme

Threads were also used to seek revenge. Three threads of three different colours tied with three knots with a curse placed on them could bring about disaster for the one who had given offence. Witches were notorious for making of a *corps creathe* or clay body.

> *One of the most malicious of their practices was the*
> *making of the corps creathe. When they wanted to injure*
> *or cause the death of anyone they made a clay image*
> *representing the person whom they wanted to injure and*
> *stuck it all over with pins. Then it was put in a running*
> *stream and as the flowing water wore away the clay, the*
> *person it represented withered and pined away, as if in*
> *the grip of a mortal disease; when the last of the clay was*
> *carried away by the water, the person died.*
>
> *Mythology and Folklore in Lewis,* Norman Morrison, 1925

On the marriage of his intended an unrequited lover could plait threads of different colours and tie three knots on each cursing the bridal bed. The bridegroom could nullify this curse by placing a sixpence beneath his foot and leaving his left shoe untied.

Threads were thought to have protective or curing properties if they were used in the right manner.

> *Rowan tree and red thread*
> *Gar the witches tyne their speed*
>
> Traditional rhyme

A piece of red thread was tied around the tail of a cow to ensure that she gave good milk and to guard her from witches. A thread from a rope used at a hanging and passed through the mouth of the patient was thought to be a cure for epilepsy.

A straining string or snath was made to cure a sprain in any limb. A wise woman took a long thread and folded it several times then laid it on her knee with the open ends hanging downwards. She spat on the palm of her right hand and twisted the thread for a few inches then she tied a knot. This continued until twelve knots were made. A rune was chanted and the thread deemed ready to be placed around the injured part. This was used for both people and animals.

On the death of the head of a family a lock was cut off his hair and it was nailed to the lintel of the door to retain the prosperity of the household. If a bird took human hair to build its nest it was thought that the person on whose head it grew would develop headaches or become bald but this was averted if a wreath of ivy was worn. If a child had whooping cough cuttings from its hair put between slices of bread and butter had to be given to a dog. If the dog coughed the child was cured.

Rabbits and hares were born with their eyes open. This was believed to avert the evil eye and it was popular to carry the hairy foot of those animals in a pocket as an amulet. A hair taken from a cat's tail, on a full moon, had to be drawn across a stye in the eye to cure it.

Spittle

Human spittle has always been believed to contain healing and magical properties. To spit for luck is common, and a bargain was sealed by wetting thumbs with spittle and pressing them together. The sign of the cross was made by spitting in the palm of the hand while chanting the Trinity, "In the name of the Father, the Son and the Holy Ghost." It was lucky to spit on the hearth. In some areas it was believed that a birthmark could be removed if the mother licked it for nine days.

It was also believed that spittle could reduce pain and boys regularly spat on their hands before a dose of the tawse while the same action toughened the hands for a fight. If someone tripped on entering a house they had to kiss their thumb and if a child fell the parent might say, "Come here, and I'll kiss it better" both of these actions stemming from a belief in saliva's curative properties.

Men spat on the floor on meeting and sailors and fishermen spat on a coin and tossed it overboard on setting out to sea. It was lucky to spit on the first coin ever earned, while spitting on the palm of the hand and making the sign of the cross with the thumb and closed fingers averted evil.

Metal

The blacksmith was a man of importance who worked with two elements which were held in awe by ordinary people – iron and fire. Since metal has always been considered an anathema to fairies, witches and the powers of darkness people through the ages were drawn to the blacksmith's shop to seek the protection they felt there. Children were baptised and couples married *owre iron* and sick children were taken there to be cured by being threatened with a hammer.

Objects made of metal were thought to be lucky. Horseshoes were hung in byres, stables and houses for luck and caused great fear if they were not hung properly. If they swung downwards then the luck in the shoe would run out. Horseshoes were also nailed to the mast of a ship to save it from shipwreck. Ornamental horseshoes are available in shops and cardboard ones are given to a bride for luck. They are used in print as symbols of good luck and of marriage. Miniature horseshoes were also included amongst the trinkets which were wrapped in greaseproof paper and hidden in clootie dumplings.

Iron

Iron nails were hammered into furniture, cradles and ships to ensure protection from harm. They were also hammered into a tree to remove toothache based on a belief that pain could be transferred from the person to an object, thus bringing instant relief to the sufferer. Nails or pins were boiled in a pan as a charm against witches, while they in turn stuck pins in models of those whom they wished to harm.

Iron was sewn into the hems of garments which gave immunity from evil influences as long as the person was wearing them. If a jacket was tossed aside the protection no longer worked. It was also considered as a form of immunity from injury during battle.

A jacket, or short coat, plaited or institched with small pieces of iron was usually worn by the peasantry of the Borders in their journeys from place to place, as well as in their occasional skirmishes with the moss-troopers, who were most probably equipped with the same sort of harness.

A poker was placed upright, making a cross with the front bar of a fire, to ward off witches and this was still done into the twentieth century. It was usually explained away as helping to draw the draught but it could not fulfil that purpose.

It was often difficult to obtain the right sort of nails or planking on some of the treeless islands so islanders, when they visited the mainland, came home with a handful of nails or wooden pegs which they carefully hoarded until they were needed to make a coffin.

Gold and silver

A good milk yield was ensured by milking through a gold wedding ring and a stye could be cured by rubbing it with a gold ring and gold earrings were believed to cure poor eyesight. Silver was thought to give water magic properties. A silver coin was nailed to the wheelhouse of a ship to ensure a good catch.

Coins

Coins were also used as lucky charms. Silver sixpences and threepenny bits had holes pierced in them and were worn as bracelets and necklaces. A sixpence worn beneath a foot in a shoe warded off evil powers.

The seller of goods gave a luckpenny, a portion of the cost returned to the buyer to ensure a lucky bargain. This custom still exists, especially in farming areas, when beasts are sold at market. When a handbag or purse is given as a gift it was customary to place a coin, preferably silver, inside for luck. Lucky pennies were carried in a pocket but had no effect unless the garment was worn. . . If it was laid aside the luck went with it. A black sixpence was supposed to ensure continued wealth but many feared that it came from the devil

Coins were sometimes baked in oatcakes and the cake was cut up by the father. Each child was blindfolded and chose a piece, the one finding the coin received the gift of a lamb.

Coins also had curative powers: a coin placed beneath a bandage over a boil was said to cure it and a copper coin placed on a stye makes it vanish.

Clothing

In the Middle Ages a glove held out on the tip of a spear pointed to a defaulter who had broken a promise this is reflected in the custom of a pair of gloves being given to a lady at Leap Year if the man she chose to marry refused her. In the same way throwing down a gauntlet was seen as a challenge to fight; it is still usual if anyone accidentally drops a glove not to thank the person who retrieves it as this will bring bad luck to both.

It is unlucky to fan a fire with a skirt or apron because the daughter of the blacksmith who made the nails for the Crucifixion did so. If a garment is accidentally put on back to front or outside- in it is unlucky to change it, it had to be worn that way or changed for another garment altogether.

Fishermen will not wear clothes dyed with crotal because it clings to rocks and would not let them surface should they fall overboard.

Moonstruck

The influence of the moon was thought to be strongest when it was full and the timing of many actions was based on the waxing and waning of the moon. On seeing a new moon women inclined their bodies towards it three times and gave thanks to God. Turning the coins in a pocket for luck should take place immediately the new moon was spotted. If no coins were available a gold ring was turned three times and a wish made. It was unlucky if the new moon was first seen through glass.

On seeing the new moon kissing the nearest woman was thought to bring luck, as was kissing the hand three times and bowing. Getting in a fankle by putting the right hand around the left foot then making the sign of the cross on the palm with spittle while chanting the Trinity was supposed to ensure success for a new venture. Moonlight has always been considered romantic and courting was often carried out in the pale moonlight after the day's work.

Charms and incantations

Many pagan chants were Christianised and are still in use, especially in the Western Isles. To be really effective actions had to be accompanied by chants, often known only to a chosen few, especially seers and herb wives. Some sayings became household phrases such as "God save us" and "God bless you" and in certain areas "Luck be to the house" or "Hail to the house and household" which was said upon entering at all times. A specific incantation used for the protection of those about to go to war was known as a sean.

Lucky and unlucky may be abstract terms but great care was taken to increase the chance of good luck.

WORK

Work, whether on the land or at sea, in factories or shipyards, has throughout the ages gathered its own customs. The rhythm of the seasons was very important in most industries, determining what work could be accomplished and the use of natural light determined the length of the working day.

The initiation of new blood and the completion of apprenticeship led to tricks and ceremonies usually accompanied by toasts and drinking. Many of the rites begun centuries ago still survive in some recognisable form in present times.

The need to ensure success and safety led to formal behaviour which if broken or neglected by any member of a crew or gang was believed to bring the possibility of disaster to others and was a serious offence.

Placating the old gods led to taboos, avoidance of unlucky practices and people, and immediate action to counteract the influence of evil associated with them. Belief in the reality of evil influence pervaded all walks of life and every precaution was taken to prevent accidents or disaster.

Most industries, especially crafts, liked to foster a sense of intrigue, to have their secrets, known only to those in the inner sanctum and gradually reveal these to new members under strict penalties if they spoke of them outwith the craft. The tools of the masons are still the basic symbols of

Freemasonry and the ceremony of the Horseman's Word has been preserved in many areas.

Farming

Until mechanisation in the second half of the twentieth century farming remained thirled to its old ways. Every act from springtime until harvest had its own customs. Animals were constantly watched for signs that the witches, fairies or a glance from an evil eye had harmed them or drawn off their milk. Dairying was beset with problems which could be remedied only by careful attention to custom and ceremonies had to be carried out to the letter to ensure success. There is still a deep-seated belief, often unacknowledged, that the powers of evil do exist and can cast their influence on the land and the weather.

Ploughing

It was considered favourable for ploughing to begin when the moon was on the wane. Several ceremonies accompanied the act of making the first opening in the earth, streaking the plough being amongst the most common. A morsel of the last sheaf cut on the previous year, was given to the horse drawing the plough and a drink and some food, usually bread and cheese, to the ploughman, who in turn toasted the farmer and his family.

In some areas the farmer also drank a glass of beer or whisky, filled it again and poured it over the bridle of the plough, saying, "G'weed speed the labour," or "God speed the plough," depending on the area. This acted as a blessing and no further work was carried out that day, a supper and dance often being held in the barn at night to celebrate. At this supper a ring was hidden in the brose and whoever found it would be the first to marry.

There was generally a six-week lay-off from ploughing in winter. To discover if the earth was ready for ploughing again, in Argyll, it was turned over and small sticks were placed in it. They were later pulled from the earth and sniffed and by their smell the soil was declared ready or not. Good Friday was thought to be an unlucky day for ploughing

In the Highlands earth from the first furrow was rubbed over the horse's neck and shoulders. On Islay the horse's ears were stuffed with butter on the first day of the ploughing season and in the Lowlands the harness, plough and horse's ears were sprinkled three times with salt water.

Sowing

The seed was often steeped in water prior to sowing then placed on a basket on top of an egg and an iron nail which was thought to ensure germination, upon which the harvest's success depended. Blessings and prayers for its fertility were also said. The sowers walked sunwise to sow the seed from a triangular cloth or later a basket hung around their necks.

St John's Eve

On St John's Eve, June the twenty fourth, farmers lit a heather torch from the bonfire. To ensure good crops it must stay allight while it was carried round the circumference of the field. Young people jumped through the embers to be blessed. Everyone then joined in the dancing until dawn.

Harvesting

The climax of the farming year was the Hairst. The bringing in of the harvest, especially if it was a good one, was a time of great celebration and ritual. As the reapers gathered they drank a toast and the farmer would lay his bonnet on the ground, lift his sickle, face the sun and cut a small handful of corn. This was moved sunwise three times around his head and a chant set up as a blessing on the harvest. The harvesters worked in teams and a kiss could be claimed from the girl bandster, who made the bands to tie the sheaves, if the band broke.

Last sheaf

There were celebrations when the last sheaf was cut. The shearers lined up and threw their sickles at the last stalk of grain, as in the Highlands it was considered unlucky to know who cut it. In the Lowlands, however, it was an honour when the "hare" was cut and a race took place to win a special dram from the farmer. In Minnigaff, the reapers would race to the farm, the winner being the first to marry. In other areas it was placed above the door and the Christian name of the first person to enter would be that of the future spouse of whoever had cut it.

The last sheaf was called a maiden if the harvest was early and the cailleach if it was late. There was a variety of customs connected with this important sheaf. Often it was dressed like a maiden with ribbons and finery and took pride of place at the Clyack or little winter feast, held to celebrate the completion of the cutting and before the kirn, and toasts were drunk to her. Part of the sheaf, a fertility symbol, was kept until the first horse had foaled as it was thought to represent new life, and another part might be buried beneath the first furrow ploughed so that the fertility might be transferred.

Corn dollies

Corn dollies were made from the sheaf also. The name stems from the word idol and there are many different patterns used such as the horn of plenty. They are thanks offerings for a fruitful harvest and are not peculiarly Scottish although certain of the shapes are more commonly found here. Small versions were given by young men to their sweethearts and one farmer would send a dolly to his neighbour to announce that his harvest was completed. They were often hung over the lintel of a door for luck.

Kirn

The kirn was the Scottish celebration of harvest home, a monumental feast with a special brew called "meal and ale" which was a lethal punch served in a bowl into which trinkets had been placed.

> *You dove in wi' yer speen tae see what ye could get, gin ye got a ring ye were likely tae get a man and gin ye got the button there was little hope for ye. . . an a saxpence was still a saxpence and could pit a bit ribbon in yer hair or gin ye were a man pit a bittie tobacco in yer pipe.*
>
> The Cornkister Days, David Cameron, 1984

It was a night of romance and dancing for the young,repeated throughout the area, as each farm finished and invited the neighbours to celebrate with them.

Harvest Sunday

On this Sunday, still celebrated in most kirks, a sheaf of corn decorates the pulpit and the congregation bring if not the actual fruits of their harvest, a selection of food, tinned and fresh, for distribution to the less fortunate.

Shepherds

At Beltane shepherds cut a circular trench and lit a fire of sacred wood. They made a caudle of eggs, butter, oatmeal and milk, spilling some on the ground to ensure the safety of their flock in the coming season and to placate the old gods. They drank it with beer and whisky. Often an oatcake was baked with nine raised knobs dedicated to various deities and each shepherd broke off a piece and said, "This to thee, preserve thou my sheep."

In Stirlingshire, they cast lots to determine which two of shepherds would became the Keepers of Beltane. It was their job to hide away the cake until the following Sunday when they would break up the oatcake and blacken one piece in the fire. The company were blindfolded and chose a piece of oatcake and the one who drew the burned one then leapt three times through the flames in continuation of a Druidic custom when the chosen one might in reality have been sacrificed to the God of Light.

Shepherds made a hoop of rowan and passed the lambs through this to keep them safe from the evil eye. On quarter days when special bannocks were baked and toasted in front of a fire of sacred wood the dry meal left over on the baking board was gathered and placed in a footless stocking, and then sprinkled over the sheep for protection. A magic word or charm was often sewn into the waistcoat or bodice of the shepherd or shepherdess for the same purpose.

Herdsmen

Cattle were made to pass through the smoke of the Beltane fire on May the first in order to cleanse them. This custom came from the Druids and was eventually Christianised as protection from evil in God's name and to guard against sickness or murrain. At one time cattle, especially bulls, were sacrificed at Beltane and it was thought to be particularly effective if there was a crescent moon. This was also the time in the Highlands when the flocks were taken to the shielings or summer pastures. Anyone meeting the procession had to give them a blessing. The evening of the arrival at the pastures a shieling feast was held where lamb was usually served and ale drunk. Charms were supposed to have extra powers at Beltane and the cattle were often blessed and sprinkled with urine.

Dairying

The byre was usually protected from evil by placing a variety of magic or sacred twigs and plants above the door. Cattle were taken to the bull on the first and third quarters of the moon but never at a neap tide. If a cow took ill it was attributed to someone having praised it or having counted the herd without adding "Luck fare the beasts." A newborn calf had dung put into its mouth to ward off evil.

In many farms the milkmaids left a bowl of cream for the brownie or goblin who was believed to live in the byre. A coin was placed at the bottom of a milk cog to prevent curdling.

Milk was poured out on to hollow stones and left for the fairies, while on Jura, a coggie of milk was taken to the hill and poured on the fairy circles. A hoop of marigold and dandelion bound with lint was placed beneath the milkpail to prevent the milk thinning. Sometimes figwort, cut on an incoming tide, or a bag with an iron nail and a piece of pearlwort was used for this purpose. Whichever was chosen it had to be carried three times around the pail deaseil before being put into place.

One farmer was appointed to inspect and try another's cream if there was a suspicion that it might be bewitched. To prove that it was "honest milk" a penny was laid gently on the surface of the cream, if it sank all was well but if it sat on top the farmer was accused of draining the cream away from a neighbour's milk by supernatural means.

Butter and cheese making

Farmers' wives prided themselves on being expert butter and cheese makers and they usually supervised the dairy even in prosperous farms. If butter was being made and a visitor entered the milk-parlour they were invited to take a hand in the process or the milk might curdle and the butter refuse to set. This was also blamed on the evil eye, horse hair or in the eighteenth century a frog was sometimes put into the churn to make it set, a practice reflected in the saying "If the butter has no hair in it the cow will not thrive." It was considered unlucky to wash the churn, a habit frowned upon by the more hygienic visitors from the south.

If it was believed that a witch had deliberately cursed the dairy then pins were boiled in a pan and a charm recited and she was supposed to suffer pain and recant releasing the spell. Witches were placated by leaving dishes of groats or a supply of peat or thatch for them. Cheeses – "kebbocks" were made for all celebrations and "new" made cheese was eaten as an antidote to poison.

Tattie-maiden

At the end of the potato lifting a maiden was made from the shaws in the form of a cross which was carried at the front of the Grand March, in which everyone took part, at the beginning of the dancing.

Blackmail

The Highlanders often raided the lowlands to demand money and cattle. If these were not willingly given they set fire to the crops and on occasions even burned down the farmhouse. This protection money was known as blackmail.

Gudeman's croft

The name Gudeman's croft was given to that part of each field which was never cut and the grass was allowed to grow high as a shelter for the fairies or brownies.

Fishing

Fishing has always been a dangerous and uncomfortable way of life and this possibly explains why ritual has been observed throughout the centuries, giving a sense of security which can be equated with safety. The coastal communities of the North-East, Angus, Fife and the Lothians as well as those on the west coast were close knit, sometimes claustrophobic in their way of life. Incomers from a non-fishing background found their ways foreign and well nigh incomprehensible.

Traditions and customs were slavishly followed and those who broke them, even unintentionally, were frowned upon and accused of endangering the lives of others. The building and launching of a boat and the actions of the crew, on land as well as at sea, were tied to a series of customs and beliefs which were deep-seated and of extreme importance.

Celebrations were held to mark the end of the salmon season when free smoked salmon was served in public houses and horse races took place, while regattas were held at the close of the cod fishing. On Christmas Day any fish caught were given as gifts to widows and orphans.

Building a boat

A new boat was a major purchase and represented an investment for future success so everything possible had to be done to ensure that it would be a lucky boat. The choice of wood was important, sacred or magic woods being best. It was believed that boats made of she-oak sailed faster at night than any other and the use of aspen or other crossed woods had to be avoided at all costs. Wood from a tree which grew near the grave of an unbaptised child was never to be used as it was believed that the ghost of the child would haunt the ship.

It was considered unlucky to use old wood in building a new boat. The grain of the wood used for decks was studied with a keen eye: swirling shapes foretold disaster while knots shaped like fish promised successful fishing. A red thread was tied around the first iron nail and at Portnockie on the Moray Firth the owner's wife put on the first mop of tar for luck but the mop had then to be stood upright and never left head down. The main mast received particular attention and a gold sovereign was buried beneath it plus a horseshoe nailed to it for luck. Keels were never laid down on a Friday nor were boats commissioned on that day.

Launching a boat

Barley was sprinkled on the deck for luck and successful fishing. The boat had to have touched water before the traditional blessing of "May God bless this boat and all who sail in her" was uttered and the bottle of wine or champagne was broken across her bow. Boats are always referred to as "she" and this led to the belief that it was unlucky to sail with a woman aboard because the boat might be jealous and take revenge.

Friday and Monday were to be avoided for launches as was the day of the week on which the keel was laid. In Portessie the company would gather round the new boat and cheer as beer was thrown over the vessell, then they chanted her name. Afterwards a boat feast was held with beer and whisky and bread and cheese.

Nets

When nets were being mended on land they were sprinkled with whisky and the crew members were given a dram when the task was completed. No woman, especially a bare-footed one, should step over the nets or they could not be used. Nets were not be touched on the Sabbath or the herring would flee. In St Monance the nets were washed in a magic spring dedicated to St. Monan because it was believed that iron in the water toughened them. Here also the church bell was never rung if a shoal of herring was sighted in case it would frighten them off. If on preparing a line an unlucky person entered the house the end of the line had to be drawn through fire to cleanse it.

At sea

If it was the first outing of the boat after the close season a bottle of whisky was broken over the bow to hansel it and bring luck and the deck was sprinkled with holy water. The crew boarded the boat from the right side and the boats always left harbour in a sunwise direction even if this was more awkward. A silver coin was spat on and tossed over the bow for luck and no-one could ask where they were going.

If a salmon leaped in front of the boat it would turn back. Another boat could not be pointed at directly nor referred to by name and no-one on shore was to call after them. The clouds were studied to read the weather omens and sighting various birds was considered lucky or unlucky.

> *Wild geese, wild geese, gangin' to the sea,*
> *Good weather it will be.*
> *Wild geese, wild geese, gangin' to the hill,*
> *The weather it will spill.*
>
> Traditional

Curlews were an omen of death or shipwreck and seagulls were thought to be the souls of the dead who had drowned at sea. Swallows were a sign of good weather.

No bread was cut until the lines were out or the haddock might be eaten by the dogfish. The words fish or fishing were avoided and the first fish caught was generally thrown back to placate the sea god, Shony.

Bread cast upon the water

On festival days such as St Michael's Day and Hallowmas gruel and ale were cast on the waves as an offering to the old gods. In some areas the priest or minister blessed the nets and prayed that they might be filled. The god of the sea was called Shony and was respected and honoured with church services in many fishing villages begging Shony to provide for them. The congregation then proceeded to the shore where one fisherman would wade out into the sea with a cup of home-brewed ale saying:

> Shony I give you this cup of ale hoping you will be so kind as to send us plenty of sea-weed for enriching our ground for the coming year.

Traditional

They returned to the church where a candle burned and put out the flame. Celebrations followed, usually in a field where the population would feast, sing and dance until dawn.

Casting lots

On Barra on St Bride's Day the fishermen cast lots for the fishing banks. Each area was divided into sections and men only fished in their designated area. There were three seasons: Doon-drawin at Beltane, Johnsmas at Midsummer and Foy at Lammas when the fishing season closed and the men returned home to tend to their land.

Taboos

Egg shells could not be left in two but were always crushed

so that witches could not use them to raise storms. Wives never washed clothes on the day their men went to sea as the action might wash him away. On setting out for the boat there were people and things best avoided. Meeting a red-haired women, a minister or priest, a chimney sweep or anyone with a squint or who was flat-footed made the fisherman turn back and postpone his journey unless he went through the house and came out of the back door backwards. If his path was crossed he could take out his knife and draw the sign of the cross saying, "Twee-to-see-die" and then spit. Customs can become obsessions and when every member of the crew had to observe them it was a wonder that the boats ever put to sea.

Lucky encounters

There were lucky encounters also. If fire was carried three times around a fishing boat on Hogmanay it brought luck or in Shetland if one of "Gude's Poor", that is a simple or crippled person, crossed their path it was a good omen. If the catch was good such people were given money on the boat's return. Sometimes a lucky person was asked to cast off the ropes as the boats left shore, while in Auchmithie the womenfolk carried their men on their backs to and from the boat.

Taboo words

In every fishing area there was a variety of alternatives to unlucky words. Pigs were called cauld-iron beasties in Fife, grunters and curly-tails elsewhere. No member of a crew should mention kirk or minister, pig, rabbit, hare, fox or rat. In Cullen the names Duffus and Anderson were thought unlucky and were never spoken. If any taboo words were uttered cold iron had to be touched immediately such as the studs on their clogs.

Salt was another unlucky word. It was needed at sea but must never be borrowed on a Monday. If spilled it must be thrown over the left shoulder to avoid ill-luck.

Lucky and unlucky items on board

White-handled knives and white pebbles were thought unlucky, while bringing on board Swan-Vesta matches was frowned upon because the swan was thought to be an unlucky bird. A bannock which was baked on Shrove Tuesday or Good Friday was very lucky indeed. A caul from a child was prized as a talisman against drowning and gold earrings were worn for the same purpose. A piece of coal and a cowrie shell were considered lucky, and a piece of red flannel, which was supposed to cure a sore throat, was often found amongst a fisherman's accoutrements.

Wind

The wind was very important to anyone who went to sea. If a fisherman was walking along a street and saw leaves whirlling in a circle he would throw a shoe at them to frighten away the fairies and make them drop anything which they might have stolen. There were two distinct problems at sea, some customs were used to clam the storm and others to provide a wind to fill the sails. To calm a the waves a hand was waved gently in the opposite direction from the swell of the waves. Figureheads on ships were usually barebreasted depictions of women as this was thought to calm the waves. It was believed that if a body went overboard the sea would not be calm until it was recovered. The word pig was taboo because saying it brought on a storm. Whistling on board ship was forbidden for the same reason. If sealskin was wrapped around the mast it calmed the sea.

If the ship became becalmed then it was permissable to whistle gently to bring up a wind. On Barra fishermen called out to St Brendan to stir up a wind and if a steel-bladed knife was stuck into the mast in the direction from which the wind was desired it would blow up.

Sabbath Observance

Nets were not prepared and boats never went to sea on a

Sunday. The fishermen waited until midnight or early Monday morning to sail.

Craftsmen

Apprentices can take several years before becoming a journeyman. While this approach to work is now diminishing there were many customs associated with it.

Guilds were set up in the Middle Ages and the Church of Rome gave every craft a patron saint. Pageants were held in celebration of each particular saint's day but these were banned by the Presbyterians after the Reformation. Apprentices had to pay dues to support the craft's altar in the local church.

Building trade

A founden pint of beer was given to the workmen on the site when the first foundation stone was laid. Mortar mixed with the blood of a bull was at one time poured into the first cut and beer may be poured into it for luck. There is often an official ceremony carried out by a personality or dignitary to lay the first stone of a new building. Topping out is a ceremony to celebrate the last stone or brick of a building being put into place. A silver trowel is often presented after this ceremony to the person who carried it out. This was followed by feasting and a dram was offered to the workers. If this was not freely given the building might be cursed and lie empty or be unlucky.

The custom of tossing the caber at Highland games stems from a method of house building prevailing in the Highlands where tree trunks were tossed upright to form the walls.

Miners

Like fishermen miners had a list of lucky and unlucky people to meet on the way to work and would turn back and set out again should such a person cross their path. They refused to go back if they had forgotten something as that would bring bad-luck.

Miners did not like the sign of the cross to be seen underground and avoided leaving tools lying crossed. If an accident occurred all work would immediately stop and no miner would return to the same seam if a mate was killed underground; they avoided the area, believing that the ghost would haunt the pit until the funeral. The miners collected food, clothing and money to give to the widow whose husband had met with an accident and left it anonymously on her doorstep.

Deal money

Money often changed hands on sealing a bargain, usually accompanied by a jar of ale or a glass of whisky to moisten the deal. A hairst fee, for example, was given by the farmer to the hired hand at the feeing fair and a barber, or croppit man, was paid in drams or ale silver. He would give back a penny for the weans. When a piece of land was sold the buyer gave the wife of the owner a ring or an other small gift which came to be known as the wife's interest.

Apprentices in work such as textile printing had to fork out ale money on completion of their first piece and at various times throughout their training to provide drink for the journeymen. This was served in a communal bucket into which the men dipped their cup and might be the origin of the saying "He takes a good bucket" often applied to heavy drinkers.

In shipbuilding "whisky foremen" expected those looking for work or those grateful to be working to pay for a dram for them at the local public house.

Women and song

Women were fellow workers at farming and fishing and many worked in the textile industries both at home and later in factories. The one custom which was common to all forms of work was singing which is mentioned regularly as an adjunct to the work and in many oral histories it is this aspect which is remembered with pleasure.

Originally songs, such as those for waulking cloth, provided rhythm for the work and helped the workers to keep in step. Even when weaving began in factories the workers would pass the day singing. It was common among women who worked in the munitions factories during both world wars although by then it was popular songs rather than the traditional airs which were sung.

Initiation

One area in which nearly all occupations took a delight was in the initiation both of newcomers, especially youngsters at their first job, and of apprentices becoming journeymen on completion of their time.

These occasions were marked by tricks, rituals and drink. The lad on his first morning in the farm bothy would be awakened at 5 a.m. by having a sweaty sock drawn across his face and on rising might find that his bootlaces were tied together or his trouser legs sewn up. A crowd might have gathered on a bridge beside a river to watch a youngster catch his first illegal trout and be initiated as a poacher, The trickiest part being to keep his nerve as the water-bailie passed along. On his first morning in a shipyard the apprentice had to suffer the humiliation of being sent for a long stand, a left-handed screwdriver or striped paint.

When the apprenticeship was finished it was a time for celebration. This always seemed to involve the dirtiest, messiest product of the trade being smeared all over the recipient and marching around banging and rattling and making as much noise as possible while consuming a large quantity of drink. Coopers were smeared with oil and wood shavings, put into the barrel and doused with beer and rolled around.

Brothering was a seafaring tradition which took place on land, in a pub with the newest crew member being stood in front of everyone with a noose around his neck. He was forced to eat a roll filled with salt and had beer thrown on his face by the skipper and water over his legs by the firstmate. The beer represented the spume over the bow and the water the sea crashing over the deck. The skipper recited

> *From St. Abbs Head tae Flamborough Head,*
> *Whene'er ye cut, be sure ye bend,*
> *Ne'er lea' a man wi' a loose end.*

Traditional

Another ploy was to daub the face of the newest crew member with soot and grease while asleep and then take him ashore. He, being oblivious, suffers guffaws of laughter. Tricks like this were usually carried out ashore where there were more people to enjoy them. Aboard ship it is still a ritual when crossing the equator for the first time for a seaman to have his face lathered and be ducked in the ship's pool or in a basin by King Neptune himself.

When a farmhand became fully fledged his gang siezed him under the arms with his feet barely touching the ground or carried him shoulder-high astride a wooden pole twice around the square before tossing him into the hotel bar where he had to stand drinks for the company. This was called a Clugston.

Horseman's Word

In the bothies of the North-East and in other parts of Scotland ritual ceremonies were held in secret to impart the Horseman's Word to the initiate. This Word was supposed to give control over any horse, bending it to the horseman's will to bring down the horse of an enemy. One version required the initiate to sit alone at midnight in an empty loft with no other person within call and to eat a half loaf of bread and drink a bottle of whisky, after which the devil appeared and gave him the Word. In Buchan four horsemen were with the novice who had to supply the loaf, whisky and a candle. He was blindfolded and led to the altar, which was usually a sack of corn. He was questioned, had to take an oath and then shook the devil's hand and was given the Word.

It was like a masonic ceremony and was taken very seriously. The initiate promised not to write, carve nor divulge the Word to anyone under penalty, "May my flesh be torn to pieces with a wild horse and my heart cut through with a horseman's knife and my bones buried on the sands of the seashore where the tide ebbs and flows." The devil was usually a stick covered in animal hair or even a person dressed up, but the atmosphere was realistic and convincing.

WATER

Water in all its manifestations was regarded as sacred by the Druids and as magical by the peasantry who used it as the panacea for all ills. Every gift from the earth proved that a guardian spirit lived within and should be appeased by offerings. The Celts threw gold and silver into sacred pools. The Roman Church decided that if it could not wean people away from their beliefs they, in turn, would sanctify those wells which were regularly visited and dedicate them to the local saint and declare the water holy. St Columba is recorded as having blessed over three hundred water sources in the Highlands and Lowlands.

Most churches and holy places are built close to where such wells were in existence. Although the Presbyterians declared the practice of visiting wells idolatrous they could not stamp it out. The General Assembly of the Church of Scotland was outraged when in 1560 it discovered that the kirk of Restalrig was built over the covered well of St Triduana, which had been a place of pilgrimage for over a thousand years, and demanded that it be razed to the ground.

Rivers, lochs, burns, pools and wells all had their devotees who swore that amazing cures for all disease and protection from harm could be obtained by visiting these places and carrying out the correct actions. Offerings had to be made to ensure success and even in Presbyterian times a variety of objects: stones, bones, beads and coins were sacrificed. In Victorian times hydropathics and spas were built in areas where the water was considered especially curative.

That some of the cures appear today more torturous than the affliction did not seem to worry our ancestors who submitted to them gladly, ensuring that the rites associated with each one were studiously observed. In fact, minerals coming from the depths of the earth did often have properties which were beneficial and, as people observed an invalid getting better, this reinforced the belief in the magical power of the water.

Wells

Not every well was visited for the same purpose. There were clootie wells, where wishes were made, healing wells whose water cured all or specific illnesses, wells which enabled people to see through mist, wells which granted protection from evil or fairies and wells which encouraged fertility. Cattle were protected and infants baptised with water taken from certain wells. Additions were made to wells to ensure added strength, such as the skull of a suicide thought to make the water effective in the cure of epilepsy.

Not all wells were beneficial. Drinking from the Borgie Well near Cambuslang was considered a dangerous thing to do since it was reputed to bestow rather than cure madness.

A drink from the Borgie,
A bite of the weed.
Sets a' the Cams'lang fouk,
Wrang in the heid.
　　　　　Traditional

Another well which resented strangers was the Fivepennies Well on the Isle of Eigg. If someone who was not a native slept overnight beside this well they developed a deformity in some part of their body.

Timing

Wells were visited before setting out on a journey and bannocks were baked for special occasions with water from a sacred well. The effect of the water was strongly influenced by timing. Sunrise or just before was the time of day when the powers were at their best. The influence of the moon was also taken into account and the healing powers were thought to be strongest towards the end of its first quarter.

Clootie wells

The correct approach to a clootie well, as to any other, was from the east on the southern side. Three handfuls of water were taken and drunk in silence and a wish made which must not be revealed. A piece of material was then tied to the branch. No-one should remove a rag from the tree because the troubles of the person who put it there adhered to it and were transferred.

On the Black Isle, near to Munlochy, there are two wells, the Craigie Well and St Boniface's Well. At both the trees are afire with colour from the rags which visitors tie on the branches close to the clootie well. Those wanting a cure had to take three handfuls of water from the well and spill it on the ground. They then tied a piece of cloth to the tree, made the sign of the cross and drank from the well.

Healing wells

People took the sick to wells to seek a cure for a wide variety of diseases despite the Kirk's disapproval. They usually walked or were carried three times deaseil around the well and then immersed themselves in the water if it was not an underground spring. If the water was to be drunk it should first be silvered by placing a coin in it. Sore eyes were soothed, deafness relieved, chest illness cured. Asthma was the prerogative of St Aidan's Well, in Angus, chincough or whooping cough at St Medana's Well, Monreith, in Galloway. It is recorded that:

*Magrat Davidson, spous to Andro Adam, fined £5.00
[Scots] for sending her child to be washed at St Fiacre's
Well and leaving an offering.*

Kirk Session Minutes, Aberdour, 1630

In Edinburgh, St Catherine's Well was covered at times with
a black substance to which people came in the hope of curing
skin diseases. As this was caused by seams of coal seeping into
the water it may well have had a beneficial effect.

In the Middle Ages leprosy sufferers were forced to seek
refuge in remote areas. The Well of the Rees in Galloway, an
open pool spouting from the earth beside three standing
stones, may have been near a leper colony.

Children who were suffering from wasting diseases were
swaddled in a plaid, tied to a stake and made to spend the night
alone on Therdy Hill, Inverness-shire, beside a well. To some,
cures were attributed to the fact that Therdy Hill was a fairy
knoll, and the fairies recovered the real child and took away the
changeling whom they had substituted many years before.

In North Uist on a hill there is a well near the shielings.
Those wanting a cure from toothache had to go to the well,
and not speak, eat or drink until reaching the well, where they
had to drink three handfuls in the name of the Father, the Son
and the Holy Ghost.

A wooden image of St Fumac was taken on May the third
every year and washed in his well by its custodian and the
water used to heal the sick. Also in Banff the head of St
Marnock was at one time preserved and carried in procession
to obtain fair weather. It was washed every Sunday at his well
and the water was much sought after for its healing
properties.

Cheese wells

People setting out on a journey made an offering of cheese to
a well in order to be able to see in the mist and to prevent them
from getting lost. There is a cheese well near Inverness. Barley
cakes were sometimes left beside a well to discover whether a

patient would recover from an illness. If they were neglected by the fairies or witches it was a sign of an impending death.

Baptismal water

Water was taken from wells known to have sacred properties for the baptism of infants. In Aberdeen water was always collected from St Machar's Well to put into the baptismal font at the nearby cathedral. Mothers took back-gane or ailing children to St Fillan's Well in Renfrewshire to be baptised with the water. A fisherman's son had to have his hand baptised in the waves before his twenty-first birthday to avert death from drowning.

Cattle

Cattle and other beasts were blessed with well water sprinkled over them and their harness. Sometimes shackles and other parts of the harness were hung on a nearby tree and sprinkled The Stot Well was famous for curing the connach, a wasting disease in cattle.

Votive offerings

Coins, needles and pins and other objects were thrown into wells as offerings to placate the spirit. In many areas a sacred tree grew beside the well and people would push coins into its bark. Queen Victoria in 1877 is supposed to have placed silver coins in the bark of the tree which grows beside the wishing well dedicated to St Mourie on Loch Maree. Coins from some wells such as the one at Culloden began to be collected and given to charity and this in itself became a custom. People threw coins in to a well or even a man-made fountain and made a wish, knowing that they were contributing to a good cause.

Pilgrimages

These were a great excuse for feasting and jollity especially on the Quarter Days which fell in summer and autumn and on the first Sunday in May folk would set out in their droves to pay homage at the nearest holy well. Such a pilgrimage was the equivalent of a holy fair, which was the secular name for the communion services held out of doors and celebrated in verse by Robert Burns.

> *In spring there met round the little wells at Moffat a throng, in their gayest and brightest, from society in town and country, sipping the unpleasant waters and discussing their pleasant gossip. At the bowling green were to be seen sauntering valetudinarian city clergy, men of letters, and country gentlemen, ladies of rank and fashion; while the diseased, decrepit, of the poorest rank, who had toilsomely travelled from far off districts to taste the magic waters, loitered in their rags in the village street.*
>
> The Social Life of Scotland in the
> Eighteenth Century, H.G. Graham, 1899

At Macduff, on the north-east coast every Sunday tradesmen and shopkeepers dressed in their best went down to the shore and drank quantities of sea-water from stone jugs and crystal glasses then they walked to the Well of Tarlair to drink the mineral water. In Edinburgh on May the first in the morning the people went on a pilgrimage to the well of Our Lady of Loretto at Musselburgh.

New Year water

On New Year's morning, since it was thought to be lucky, there was great competition to draw the first water from a well. If a young girl was the first she would marry that year. Farmers' wives liked to wash their dairy utensils in New Year water to bring plenty during the year, and sometimes it was given to the cows to drink to increase their yield.

Lochs

Lochs were also considered to have magical powers. The Doo Loch was noted for the treatment of palsy and other crippling diseases. Sufferers were sprinkled with water or if possible were immersed in it. Bread was left as an offering and rags were tied to a nearby tree, usually a rowan or other sacred wood. At Treval's Loch in Orkney the offerings were oatcakes and ribbons. In Strathnaver the patient had to walk backwards, dip themselves in the water, leave a coin and return to land without looking round.

Insanity

On Innis Maree, one of the twenty-seven islands in Loch Maree, there is a well dedicated to St Maelrubha which was thought to have power to cure insanity. An oak tree nearby is thick with nails where formerly cloths had hung and has coins embedded in its trunk. In more recent times the sufferer was rowed on to the loch, tied with a rope of horsehair which was placed around their shoulders and under their arms, dragged behind the boat and taken twice around the island. Once on the island they were plunged into the well and drank its water. So thorough was this cure that people came for miles to undergo the torture and be declared sane.

Columba's Loch, Benbecula received offerings in the name of St Ternan and pilgrims who came to drink the water threw leaves of the torranan plant, which grew nearby, into the loch in the hope of a cure.

Pools

In Celtic times pools were graced by specific goddesses. Latis and Coventina were the goddesses of wells, healing springs and pools. Gold and silver coins were thrown into pools to appease them and ensure good health.

At St Fillans, near Tyndrum, the pool is famed for curing insanity amongst other illnesses. Three old cairns which were opposite it were demolished and a large number of coins left by thankful people for miraculous cures was found underneath. The women bathed on one side of a rocky point and the men on the other. Each person gathered nine stones from the pool then walked up the hill to the cairns and went round each one three times sunwise, at each turn leaving a stone on the cairn. To cure a broken arm or leg an item of clothing which covered it had to be places on the cairn. Huge crowds came here to bathe especially on the end of the first quarter of a new moon.

The cure for insanity was more dire. The person afflicted was tied to a rope and plunged into the water of the pool. They had to lift three stones from the bottom of the pool and place them on the cairns which they walked round sunwise. They were then taken to the old priory where they were tied up and left alone all night in a cleft rock and fastened to a frame. They were covered with hay and the bell of St Fillan was put on their head. If they were found loosed in the morning the cure had worked. The bell disappeared but was recovered in 1869 and placed in the Scottish National Museum of Antiquities in Edinburgh.

On the Black Isle in a glen there was a fairy pool which the children visited in summer and dressed it with white stones and flowers to please the little people. Lovers visited Morag's Fairy Glen in Dunoon to make a wish at the wooden bridge.

Dew

Dew was considered the most sacred water of all by the Druids. May dew in particular was treasured and young girls liked to wash their faces with it to ensure beauty. It was preserved and sprinkled on cattle or ropes were soaked in it and hung in the byre to bring a plentiful supply of milk. Others used the dew as a healing substance to cure goitre, poor sight and consumption. Children who were ailing were rubbed down with it to strengthen their limbs.

In Edinburgh crowds of folk climbed Arthur's Seat on May Day morning to wash their faces in the dew. *The Daily Record* reported in 1934 over two hundred girls were on the summit. A hundred years earlier a maypole was erected and dancing took place but this custom died out. Church services are still held on hill tops to welcome the dawn on Easter Sunday and the first Sunday in May.

Rivers

Rivers, too, were worshipped by the Druids and were believed to have their own gods and goddesses who required sacrifices to be made to them. The Spey is said to demand a human life annually as does the Tweed but the Till is more voracious.

> Tweed says to Till,
> "What gars ye rin sae still?"
> Says Till to Tweed,
> "Though ye run wi' speed,
> and I rin slaw,
> Whaur ye droon ae man,
> I droon twa"
>
> Traditional

To discover the whereabouts of a drowned person it was customary to take a loaf of bread and scoop out the inside. It was then filled with mercury and placed in the river where it floated along and hovered over the spot where the body lay. If a gun was then fired the body would surface.

Streams

Where three streams meet was always considered to be a specially potent place for magic and many courts were set up at such places to mete out justice, with a nearby tree chosen as a hanging or gallows tree. People also congregated at these confluences to drink the water as it was thought to have magical properties.

The powers of witches and fairies were broken by crossing a running stream as Robert Burns's Tam o' Shanter knew when he tried desperately to gain the bridge at Alloway. Tinkers in Perthshire carried a child suffering from whooping cough to a stream where it was carried backwards and forwards across the water for an hour to effect a cure. At Dunskey Head cave it was traditional, at the change of the moon, to take children with rickets to the stream which flowed from the well and plunge them into the cold water then dry them in the cave to cure them and in a cave on Holy Island, off Arran, St Molios Bed was used for the same purpose and the walls are carved with pilgrims' crosses.

Water from beneath a bridge where the living and the dead pass over was used as a general cure. It had to be carried home and silvered and not a word spoken until the patient has drunk it.

Spas and hydropathics

Taking the water cure became fashionable in the nineteenth century and throughout Scotland many large baronial mansions were built to satisfy the demand. Several of them are now hotels and the appellation of Hydro has been kept in name if not in spirit. The idea behind the curative powers of water goes back to Celtic times when a prince suffering from leprosy was banished and became a swineherd. He discovered that by bathing in a muddy pool his disease disappeared and from then on the Celts accepted that water had healing powers but they attributed these not to its scientific properties but to the gods.

At Moffat, where for years people had gathered to take the waters, one of the first hydropathic establishments in Scotland was built. This was followed by many others, usually on the site of a proven well and near to a railway station. The Victorians flocked to them at Peebles, Melrose, Edinburgh, Kyles of Bute, Bridge of Allan, Dunblane, Crieff and Strathpeffer, which called itself a spa.

The regime was strict, water being the main drink, and all were temperance hotels. The clients of Peebles Hydro were prescribed water from St Ronan's Well, near Innerleithen, to cure liver and stomach complaints and treatments of mud baths and seaweed were enjoyed. Similar treatments are provided at modern health farms.

Water, in all its forms, wields power over mankind and also provides a great attraction. Seaside resorts developed at first because people went to them to take a dip in the salty brine which was advised as a cure for all ills and long bamboo bath chairs were a regular sight as invalids were wheeled along.

Although nowadays most of these watering holes are visited purely for pleasure there are still coins being tossed into wells and wishes made, pieces of cloth tied on trees and mouthfuls of water surreptitiously drunk – just in case.

PLANTS AND ANIMALS

Plants and animals have been involved in customs for generations. Some are believed to be luckier than others, some have healing properties, while others must be avoided as they bring bad luck. Herbs, flowers, trees and plants, by dint of their make-up, or by reputation, have powers to heal or to ward off evil influence. Many of the cures work because they have a basis in medicine and contain beneficial substances.

Many people in the Highlands believed that diseases affecting their family or beasts were punishment for offending God or were the result of other people having a spite against them, nevertheless they had a belief in the effectiveness of a variety of cures.

Natural remedies

Plants and herbs were believed to have healing powers based on their natural properties. Their leaves and flowers were made into decoctions, concoctions, infusions, ointments and poultices to cure specific ailments and injuries. In the Dark Ages these secrets were regarded as the domain of the Druids, in the Middle Ages of the monks in their monasteries and there were always wise women who learned these secrets and who passed them down, usually just before death, to the next generation through the female line.

To be most effective the plants had to be picked, and applied, with the addition of a spoken charm and care was taken never to permit iron to come in contact with any plant or it would lose its healing power. A wide variety of plants were used for the same purpose and the choice depended on their availability.

Fevers

Mustard and garlic were given to man and beast to ward off the plague and the evil eye. The poisonous plant, hemlock, was given in small doses as a cure for cholera. Other fevers were treated with garlic and May butter, which was butter churned on May the first with a little May dew added and was preserved by the addition of salt. St John's Wort was also used to cure fever and was most effective if found by accident, especially on Midsummer's Eve. In order to lower temperature and to calm nerves violets boiled with whey, or nettles and whey, were cooled and given as a drink to the patient. Mistletoe leaves, which were reputed to remove aggression, were also used.

Cuts and bruises

Figwort which grows on the seashore and had to be cut on an incoming tide, was gathered and the leaves placed on the affected part of man or beast to cure cuts and bruises. The tuber had to be applied to sores and tumours. Sage was also used in this way. An ointment made by pounding golden rod, valerian and butter was kept to treat bruises on both man and beast.

Heart disease

Thyme mixed with honey was given internally for disorders of the heart, while infusions, made from foxgloves, were considered, correctly, to be beneficial. Motherwort was another plant believed to relieve pain from the heart.

Blood disorders

The idea of treating like with like led to a belief that if a plant gave a red juice that meant that it was good for diseases of the blood such as anaemia. Beetroot juice was considered excellent, as was rhubarb in any form and both were found in kitchen gardens. An amazing concoction called chemical food, which contained iron, was given regularly to children to build them up and this was still in use as late as the 1950s.

Headache and insomnia

Heather, boiled in water, and applied warm to the top of the head, cured headache as did dulse, made into a poultice and applied to the temples. A patient recovering from fever was washed in warm water to which chickweed was added. In addition the plant was heated and rubbed on the neck and shoulders to ensure a restful night. Eating nettles mixed with the white of egg was also a cure for insomnia.

Eyesight

Sage chewed then put into the ears of cattle or sheep who were blind recovered their eyesight. Water, drawn fresh from a well, without resting the basin on earth or stone, had to be placed on wood. Blades of grass, put into the basin of water to which a gold or silver coin was added, were then passed across the eye affected with cataract. The water was then poured into the eye to clear the sight. A paste of fern leaves mixed with white of egg and an infusion made from ivy leaves healed sore eyes.

Cough

Coughs were remedied by infusing a syrup of holly bark or a potion of harts-tongue boiled with St John's Wort and ale. The juice from ivy leaves was inhaled to relieve catarrh and thyme cured whooping cough.

Animals and birds

Animals and birds have their reputation given to them by mankind and they are labelled good or bad influences without just cause. The use of bones, hairs and horns, skin and milk of animals for the benefit of humans has brought these items into everyday custom and bestowed on them properties which they may or may not have in reality.

Clans adopted plant and animal symbols, which are still seen on their crests, to denote their occupation, such as hunting, fishing or farming. Members of the clan were never to eat the flesh of the animal which was their talisman. The clan Macdougall had a raven as its emblem. It was woven on the banner which was carried before them into battle. If it fluttered freely it was a sign that they would be victorious.

Insects

It is lucky to catch the first bee seen each year and imprison it in a purse to ensure wealth throughout the year. If a bee flew in a straight line up to someone's face they expected to hear important news that day. Although it was not known that bee stings were acid it was the custom to treat them with marigold petals. As in so many cases the action was correct even if the reason for it was unknown.

Spiders were thought of as friendly and it was customary never to kill a one or bad luck would result. A crushed spider mixed with a syrup cured a fever. Beetles were kept by children as pets and a gouldie, a beetle with a bronze back, was a very lucky possession.

Butterflies, especially white ones, were lucky to catch and keep while brown and spotted ones were unlucky, but could not be killed. If a yellow butterfly flew across a coffin it meant that the soul was safe in heaven.

Ladybirds were rarely killed because it was believed that bad luck would follow.

Fowls

Cockerels

Cockerels were buried alive in an attempt to cure epilepsy. The bird had to be black, it had to be a gift and the burial had to take place at the exact spot where the first fit occurred. If a cock crowed three times and put its head in at the door an unexpected visitor would arrive and it was usual to start preparations for hospitality on the strength of it. If a cock crowed before sunrise it was a sign that news of a death would soon be heard. Cock fighting used to be popular and was part of the festivities of Fastern's E'en, which was the day before the first day of Lent. To drink water from a well out of the skull of a cockerel was supposed to cure a variety of diseases. To cure thrush in children the blood from a cockerel's comb should be applied to the tongue with a feather from its tail.

Hens

If a hen crowed it had to be killed as this was very unlucky, but only if it was before evening worship had been held. Eggs were kept for hatching until the moon was on the wane or the chickens would be difficult to rear. Eggs laid on Good Friday were believed never to go stale and were often preserved.

Horses

If a horse neighed at the door of a house someone would fall sick. If it scratched it was the sign of a storm. If a horse died in a stable its ear should be cut off and hung in a corner to prevent the death of another animal. They often had a collar of rowan placed around their necks to guard against evil. Horses were involved in races to celebrate festivals and weddings and in the Riding of the Marches which took place in every Border town.

A white horse meant purity and goodness and when one passed it was lucky to spit on one's pinkie. To meet a piebald horse was also lucky and if two were seen one spat on the ground three times and made a wish. Finding a loose horseshoe and bringing it home to hang on the door was very lucky but to see a foal before breakfast was unlucky.

Cattle

Cattle were washed with salt water and blessed when they went to the summer pastures. It was customary to sing their favourite melodies to cattle to have them follow on or to make them easier to milk. Cows which were restive were a sign of trouble or illness in the family. If a cow fell ill it was blamed on someone casting the evil eye or else forgetting to say "Luck fare the beast". Cows were to wear a collar of rowan or ivy at night which should be passed three times through the fire before the cow goes to the bull, best timed for the waning moon of the first and third quarters.

Bulls

Because of their strength and virility bulls were revered. In the Middle Ages it was a warning of an attempt at their assassination if a bull's head was presented to a guest. Bull's blood was mixed with earth to strengthen a building. The Picts worshipped the bull, and at Burghead, Moray, there are photographs of stones with drawings of bulls. It is thought that these stones may have been ritual offerings to the sea god to ensure that he would grant fertility to the local cattle during the year. The bull was also sacrificed by the Celts in their rituals and was still being sacrificed in the Highlands as late as the eighteenth century.

Goats

Goats' milk became popular in the eighteenth century as a hangover cure for drinking too much claret. Doctors encouraged their patients to drink the whey as a tonic.

*Every year on the roads to the Highlands were to be
met elderly gentlemen on horseback, followed by their
men-servants, riding with cloak and baggage, who were
going to some wretched Highland Inn to drink modest
draughts of goats' milk.*

The Social Life of Scotland in the
18th Century, H.G. Graham, 1899

Young girls washed their faces in goats' milk and sweet violets
to become beautiful.Occasionally when lads were taking an
oath, such as the Horseman's, a goat was brought in and he
would have to ride on its back three times widdershins before
being initiated. A billy goat was hung on a ship's mast to
procure a favourable wind. On setting out if a goat crossed your
path you should turn back and leave again by the back door.

Birds

The flight of birds was studied and conclusions were drawn
as to their meaning both for weather and luck. Ravens were a
sign of death as were albatrosses when encountered at sea. It
was an unlucky omen if a bird flew into a house and over
someone's head. Magpies were unlucky if only one was seen
and doubly so if this occurred before breakfast.

*One bodes grief, two's a death,
Three's a wedding, four's a birth.*

Traditional

Some people would turn back rather than risk such bad luck
as might befall them, while others believed that they would
be in a bad mood all day. It was unlucky to hear a cuckoo
before breakfast and if one came near a house on a quarter day
it was a sign of death..

Water birds were lucky and were connected with recovery
from illness but a crane was considered evil. Swans were equated
with purity and were never killed. To see seven swans flying was
a sign of wealth and money in the pocket should be turned.

133

Trees

Wood was regarded as having its own spirit and trees were to be revered. Some woods were said to be "crossed" and were considered unlucky. The aspen should never be used for building because it was the tree on which Judas hanged himself. The people of Uist particularly disliked this tree and would not use its wood for any purpose. They even threw clods of earth and stones at it and cursed the tree. Willow wands were used by witches to cast spells on cattle and so were shunned.

Dool, or trees of sorrow, often oak or sycamore, were used as gallows trees and were avoided as uncanny. Their associated hair ropes were considered lucky for some having the power to cure leprosy if the sufferer stood under the tree at midnight.

Oak

Oak was venerated by the Druids who worshipped in sacred oak groves. It was believed to be the king of trees. The fact that it hosted the magical mistletoe gave it extra powers. Mistletoe was dedicated to the goddess of love and placed in the marriage bed as an aid to fertility. Kissing under the mistletoe may be a continuation of this belief in a different form. It was also used as an antidote to poison. The fate of the Hays of Errol in Perthshire was supposed to hang on mistletoe never deserting the oak tree.

> While the mistletoe bats on Errol's aik,
> And the aik stands fast,
> The Hays shall flourish, and their good grey hawk,
> Shall nocht flinch before the blast.
>
> But when the root of the aik decays,
> And the mistltoe dwines on its breast,
> The grass shall grow on Errol's hearthstane,
> And the corbie roup in the falcon's nest.

> Traditional ballad

It was common to swear an oath by "oak and ash and thorn" and women hugged oak trees in the belief that it would ease their delivery during childbirth. It was also a popular wood for building ships. A branch of oak, about eight inches long, called an oakum was boiled in St John's Wort and preserved in barley straw to ferment yeast. Sufferers from toothache bored a nail into their gum until it bled and then drove the nail into the trunk of an oak tree to effect a cure.

Apple

Apple trees have always been believed to be the tree of life and to have magical powers. Sleeping under an apple tree at noon on Midsummer's Day was to be avoided as the fairies might spirit you away. St Servanus flung his staff across the Firth of Forth and where it landed an apple tree blossomed. If an apple from the tree was cut in half and the seeds examined, if they were whole it was a good sign, if one was damaged it was a sign of trouble, if two seeds were damaged it indicated the death of the holder or widowhood.

Rowan

Every garden or farmyard had its rowan tree. Twigs of rowan were used to protect people and cattle and furniture, houses and boats were made from it to ensure against the influence of evil and the enchantment of witches. Carts made of rowan and tools with rowan handles were supposed to make work easier.

> *The Hags came back, finding their charms,*
> *Most powerfully withstood.*
> *For warlocks, witches cannot work,*
> *Where there is rowan tree wood.*
> > *Laidley Worm,* Traditional ballad

Patterns of rowan tree berries were chalked on doorsteps after they were washed to keep away evil spirits and this custom continued in the white chalking of stairs in tenement closes when country folk came to live and work in the towns.

Many tools in everyday use were made of rowan and pegs of rowan were used to hold parts of implements together. Necklaces of rowan were worn as a charm.

Elder

Another common tree was the elder or bourtree which guarded against evil and prevented witches from functioning. When cutting elder the pruning knife had to be spat on three times first. Handles for whips used by the driver of a horse-drawn hearse were made of elder to guard against ghosts. Many people believed that it was unlucky to burn this wood. Elderberries picked on St John's Eve, June the twenty fourth, were dried and placed on windowsills to avert evil.

Hazel

Hazel rods were favoured by diviners for detecting water buried beneath the earth. They had to be cut on St John's Day or Good Friday. Hazel was also used to cure fever and switches made of it chastised school pupils before the invention of the leather-thonged Lochgelly or tawse. The hazelnut was prized, as in the Celtic legends these nuts could make men wise. However if two nuts were present in the one shell it was unlucky to eat them.

Birch

The birch was also considered a magic or sacred wood which was brought into homes at Easter and on St John's Eve. To fell birches could bring bad luck. They were often planted in graveyards to watch over the dead and, as witches feared it, a wand of birch was placed on the coffin as a charm against their powers. Ropes for boats were often made by twisting and interlacing twigs of birch or else of fir.

Cures

Many other cures relied on natural substances. Camphor was placed in a bag and hung around the neck to cure sciatica. Salt was heated and placed in a woollen sock which was put against the face to cure gumboils or toothache. Whisky was dropped onto a sore tooth or put on a piece of cotton wool and placed in the mouth and treacle and sulphur were used to cure several ailments.

Several of the beliefs about the natural world are present today and customs such as touching wood for luck are still common. Almost all plants and herbs had their uses for one disease or another and herb gardens and physic gardens are now regaining popularity. In recent years more people are turning to natural substances for healing and alternative medicine is finding a place alongside the conventional. Life comes full circle. Old customs and new blend and for whatever reason they seem to fulfil a deep-seated need in everyday lives.

BIBLIOGRAPHY

Bennett, Margaret *Local Dimension in Oral Tradition* IN *Martin, Don* ed *Scottish Culture, The Local Dimension*, Scottish Library Association, 1991

Bennett, Margaret *Scottish Customs from the Cradle to the grave*, Polygon, 1992

Carmichael, Alexander *Carmina Gadelica*, Floris, 1994

Chambers, Robert *Domestic Annals of Scotland, vol 2, from the Reformation to the Revolution*, W & R Chambers, n.d.

Graham, H G *The Social Life of Scotland in the Eighteenth Century*, A & C Black, 1899

MacLean, Charles *The Fringe of Gold, the fishing villages of Scotland's east coast, Orkney and Shetland*, Canongate, 1985

Mactaggart, John *The Scottish Gallovidian Encyclopedia*, Clunie Press, 1981

Martin, Martin *A description of the Western Isles of Scotland circa 1685*, Birlinn, 1994

McCallum, Neil *It's An Old Scottish Custom*, Dobson, n.d.

Napier. James *Folklore or Superstitious Beliefs in the West of Scotland in This Century*, Gardner 1879

McNeill, F M *The Silver Bough, vols 1-4*, Stuart Titles, 1990

Ross, Anne *Folklore of the Scottish Highlands*, Batsford, 1976

Scott, Sir Walter *Minstrelsy of The Scottish Border*, Murray, 1869

GLOSSARY

Ae, one
aik, oak
ane, one
Auld Lang Syne, parting
   song
auld, old

Bairn, child
baith, both
bane, bone
bannock, cake of oats
   or barley
beck't, curtsied
black, unfortunate
blaw, blow
blithesome, cheerful
bobbit, moved up and
   down
bolstr, long double pillow
brawny, well built
breeks, trousers

Caller, fresh
Cam'slang, Cambuslang
cauld, cold
caup, cup
clark, secretary
clay-cauld, dead
clayis, cloth
clootie, cloth
coggie, bowl made of
   wooden staves

coronach, funeral lament
corp, dead body
cortège, funeral procession
cozie, warm
crack, gossip
creel, large basket
crook, curved staff
cry, call
cryin, labour (childbirth)

Day of obligation, religious
   holiday
deboshry, debauchery
din, noise
diseasit, diseased
Disruption, Ministers set
   up Free Church
doukin, dipping into water
dove, dived
dram, gill of whisky
drap, drop
droukit, soaked through
dung, muck,manure
dunghill, midden

E'en, evening
e'er, ever
exercised, regularly held
   family worship

Forrit, forward
fowk, folk

140

Gae, go
gall, bog myrtle
gar, make
gart, got
gied, gave
gin, if
great pencil, flag or
    pennant
gumpheon, funeral banner

Hae, has
haws, berries of the
    hawthorn
heid, head
hirdum-dirdum, uproar
hosen, stocking
hostin, coughing

Kame, comb
keening, wailing
kirk, church
kist, chest
kisting, chesting or
    coffining

Lair, a deep hole dug for a
    grave
lane, alone
learned, taught
lighter, delivered (childbirth)

Muun, must
Mess John, priest or
    minister
minny, mother
mony, many

mou, mouth
muckle, big

Or, gold
ower, over

Palladium, an item on
    which luck depends
pibroch, bagpipe music
pit, put
pluck, pull out the feathers
Possesor, God
puir, poor
pullet, young hen
pursuivants, followers

Quarter days, term or rent
    days
quey, cattle

Rapploch, undyed cloth
reeled, turned in a circle
reif, plunder
rin, run
roddin, rowan
rosemary, herb

Sackles, innocent
sain, bless
sark sleeve, shirt sleeve
sattin, satin
saulie, attendant
saut, salt
scandle, scandal
Scots, currency,
    (10/- = £1.00)

seaweed, fertiliser

seer, one who can forsee
the future

set faced, your partner

set, put

shoon, shoes

sic, such

siccan, such

sillar, silver

snaw, snow

speen, spoon

steer, stir

sten, leap

straiked, stroked

straughten, straighten

stryle, wrapped

Tap, top

theasaurer, treasurer

thrid, third

till, to

twa, two

tyne, to be

Unmortared, drystone,
without cement

Vikar, minister

Wae's, woe is

want, does not have

waukin, watching

wear, war

weel, well

wha, who

whaur, where

whinnies, gorse bushes

Yokin, a spell of work

youphing, wailing

Yule, Christmas

INDEX

NOTES